SILENT RUN!

a poetic tour of 50 UK parkrun events

by Tim Gardiner

the parkrun poet

Silent Running: stealth mode of operation to avoid detection.
Non-essential systems shut down.
Superfluous noises minimised.
Speed greatly reduced.

Dedham Vale Publishing

Poetry copyright, Tim Gardiner © 2024
Other poem authors copyright as stated

Cover photo: Sandringham parkrun © Tim Gardiner

Great Britain Aquathlon Team Captain Yiannis Christodoulou on the parkrun bug:

It all began with parkrun which opened me up to the world of running. Parkrun helped me get active without the pressure of a race. It allows people to be active and introduces them to running and from there you never know how far you can go.

Yiannis has certainly achieved plenty in the world of athletics after he started running in 2012. He was 2019 European and National Aquathlon Champion (Age Group) and competed in the 2020 European Triathlon Championships. Yiannis continues to inspire all of us that turn up on a Saturday with nothing but hope that we may complete the hallowed 3.1 miles in a quicker time than last week.

For dad

All rights reserved. No part of this publication may be reproduced, stored in a retrieval system, or transmitted, in any form, or by any means, electronic, mechanical, photocopying, recording or otherwise, without the prior permission of the publisher.

ISBN: 978-1-0369-0182-0

Published by Dedham Vale Publishing (2024)

CONTENTS

	Foreword	5
	Introduction	6
1	Severn Bridge	7
2	Hunstanton Promenade	11
3	Ganavan Sands	14
4	Chilton Fields	17
5	Sewerby	20
6	Sandringham	23
7	Harleston Magpies	26
8	Shorne Woods	29
9	Swansea Bay	31
10	Markshall Estate	35
11	Market Rasen Racecourse	36
12	Manor Field, Whittlesey	41
13	Ferry Meadows	45
14	The Cinder Track, Whitby	49
15	Monsal Trail	53
16	Storeys Field	57
17	Soham Village College	60
18	Royal Tunbridge Wells	63
19	Chalkwell Beach	66
20	Stratford-upon-Avon	68
21	Winchester	73
22	Castle Park	77
23	Conwy	80
24	North Walsham	84
25	Street	87

26	Humber Bridge	90
27	Peel	95
28	Rendlesham Forest	101
29	Wallaceneuk	106
30	Alton Water	110
31	Darlington South Park	114
32	Edinburgh	118
33	Pegwell Bay	123
34	Malling	127
35	Cassiobury	131
36	Alness	135
37	Crosby	140
38	Wickford Memorial	145
39	Mildenhall Hub	149
40	Roding Valley	153
41	Victoria Dock	157
42	Southwark	160
43	Burgess	164
44	Harrogate	169
45	Southend	173
46	Dulwich	177
47	University Parks	182
48	Belton House	186
49	Northala Fields	189
50	Fountains Abbey	193
	Appendix 1. The extra ones	197
	Appendix 2. The tourist matches	228
	Appendix 3. Parkrun poet in statistics	234

FOREWORD

Tim's poetic journey follows in the footsteps of prolific parkrun tourists. To be a parkrun tourist, you only need to visit a parkrun that is not your home event. It really is that simple. This may be one down the road or a parkrun in some far-flung corner of parkrunworld, many miles from home. Touring parkrunworld is like being given a free passport to discover (mostly) green spaces across the world that you may otherwise never have heard of.

Levels of parkrun tourism will vary depending on who you talk to. Some like to get their parkrun fix when visiting friends and relatives, many, while working away from home or on holiday (if you're lucky enough to be in a parkrun country). For others, parkrun tourism has become a game, a bit of fun added to their parkrunday, whilst for some, parkrun tourism has become an obsession. There are a few who run their first 100 parkruns each at a different venue, exploring parkrunworld as they go and never really having a home parkrun (despite being required to select one when they registered). Some even run a parkrun in every parkrun country, or run at over 500 different events! Both the parkrun show and our current podcast (With Me Now) delight in tales from parkrun tourists across the globe.

The introduction of the Running Challenges extension has fuelled the desire of many parkrunners to achieve goals they never imagined when they began their parkrun journey. As parkrun grows, so do the lengths that people will go to, using parkrun to write their adventures. The beauty of doing so is being able to tap into communities of an extended parkrun family along the way. Meeting like-minded people across the world, and being fully accepted as part of their community is magical. It was amazing for my daughter and I to experience this on our parkrun trip to Australia, New Zealand and Singapore. The world of parkrun is rebuilding a community spirit that has been fractured by modern lifestyles, and not just locally, the incredible thing about this community is that it is global. Tim's poetry tour captures the individual community spirit of each parkrun, many of which I have run with my daughter.

Nicola Forwood A8863

INTRODUCTION

My parkrun journey began at Great Notley in Essex on 7th October 2017. Cajoled into it by a work colleague, I made the classic beginner's mistake of haring around the first lap, before the 'hill of doom' did its worse. My colleague thought I was having a heart attack as she destroyed me in the sprint finish. Despite this, I soon started to tour different venues and the parkrun poetry began to flow with poems for run reports as far apart as Lincoln and Moors Valley in Dorset. The aim to reach 50 different events was achieved in the sandpit of Great Yarmouth North Beach parkrun in February 2020. The tale of the first 50 poetic parkruns was recounted in the book 'Glade Runner' released by Stour Valley Publishing in 2020.

The aim of the current book is to document, through poetry and prose, the 50 different events I've visited from February 2020 onwards towards the 100-parkrun event milestone. This journey was interrupted significantly by the long COVID-19 cessation of parkrunning. I called this book Silent Running because the 50 parkrun visits were set against a backdrop of tragic personal circumstances from which I needed a distraction and because running was much harder after the pandemic. Read on for tales of the fascinating people and places of this parkrun tour.

Tim Gardiner – the parkrun poet – A3911176

1. SEVERN BRIDGE

Run Report: View to a krill, 29/02/2020

I chose Severn Bridge for the unique Leap Day parkrun on the 29th February, a majestic location where Roger Moore's Bond would be at home in a final showdown with the bad guys. It was the first parkrun leap run, the next chance will be in 2048. Excited about the prospect of crossing from Wales to England and back again on the legendary Severn Bridge, I checked into the Severn View Travelodge off the M48. In an uncanny coincidence I had room 007; fuel to the fire of an already hyperactive mind! Sadly, I'd forgotten my passport and running watch. Neither mistake was to prove fatal, passport checks were not in operation on the border (Al Stewart wasn't available!) during the run and an iPhone was used for pacing purposes!

Nerves around the arrival of Storm Jorge and the potential closure of the Severn Bridge due to high winds, led to a poor night's sleep. Despite closure of the crossing during the night, it was open in the morning and the historic event was on. Arriving at the tunnel near the start, the mood was convivial reflected by Jonathan Carter's excellent run briefing in which the assembled mob of 181 parkrun enthusiasts was encouraged to cheer for either England or Wales! The Tunnel of Love didn't live up to its reputation with no proposals forthcoming from women as is the tradition on Leap Days, so Jonathan proposed on one knee to Julian Smith asking for his hand in co-event directing. Thankfully, to save Jonathan's blushes, Julian said yes!

Tourists came from places as diverse as Basingstoke, Bushy Park, Glossop and Manningtree in Essex (me!). Ben Whitbread completed his 50th run, while Ross Howells and Graham Taylor joined the 100 Club. There were plenty of tourists, but special mention should be made of Debbie and Paul Moulton joining the Cow (Half Cowell) Club in making Severn Bridge their 50th different event. Also present was top parkrun tourist, Becky Thurtell, completing her 533rd parkrun and 307th different event. Incredible stats and a top time of 25:17 (74:62% age grade) to boot! We had two Jeffers (run/walk method devised by Olympian Jeff Galloway) from Glossop (Gail Jazmik and Kathryn Gray), completing the windy run in respectable times for 10/2 intervals. And finally, it was noted that the average Severn Bridge run time of 29:02 spookily mirrored the Leap Day date!

Of all the events I've run so far, Severn Bridge is my favourite; it even has a siren to start runners off in Wales (Monmouthshire). The rumble of runners shook the suspension bridge cycleway, slightly disconcerting for a newcomer. We soon crossed the River Wye and leapt over the border into England (denoted by flags) on the Wye Bridge (actually separate to the Severn Bridge). Once in England (Gloucestershire), we passed over Beachley Island, with the high tree canopy providing a little respite from the gusting wind. I noticed a rifle range down below indicative of the military use of the Beachley site by the Ministry of Defence. Once you're off the Beachley Viaduct, the run progresses up the infamous Severn Loaf Hill (64 ft.) to the first tower where the bridge is around 150 ft. above the water (c. 50 m). Between the two towers was the turnaround point, expertly staffed by veteran Syd Wheeler, himself an excellent runner for age having completed 100 different parkruns. The route was lined with 19 volunteers, thanks to all of these amazing people.

Upon wheeling around Syd, the full force of Jorge was felt. I struggled back to the crest of the Severn Loaf where I was able to up the pace a little downhill before re-crossing Beachley Viaduct, the Wye Bridge and stumbling back into good old Wales.

The sprint down the heavily wooded slope towards the tunnel funnel was the easiest part of the run. Sweeping into the tunnel to the sound of a Ski Sunday style cow bell, a last ditch sprint takes you past the twinkling lights of the finish sign and the owl painted on the wall! I cannot recommend this event enough to anyone tired of their home run. It's an all-round 10/10 event from the breath-taking views of the River Wye and Severn Estuary across to the M4 Bridge, to the well organised and ultra-friendly nature of the volunteers.

Afterwards, I took the opportunity to visit Chepstow with its beautiful castle. A Welsh pigeon deposited its load on me, while the town was engulfed by rain, hail, sleet and snow in that order! It seems we were lucky to enjoy the parkrun in glorious sunshine. Perhaps the sun shone on the righteous this Leap Day morning for just one hour?

Poetry Corner

The Welsh poet, Harri Webb, famously wrote in his Ode on the Severn Bridge: two lands at last connected / across the waters wide / and all the tolls collected / on the English side. The Tolls are long gone, so my own thoughts on the bridge could be summed up, rather appropriately, in a haiku: just five kilometres / for Severn Bridge parkrunners / five on Beaufort Scale. The astronomically important day led me to write a poem for perhaps the most extreme parkrun location which may be popular with tourists in 2048!

Giant leap for ran-kind

They say stay away
from the inaugural,
this one's a must run
in a crater on the moon.
A zero-g event
walkers, joggers, runners
all content - footprints left
like Armstrong and Aldrin.
We've managed to book
a cheap return flight,
it's an early start, midweek
on low-cost EasyShutt.
On the launch pad
we check our bags,
strictly no barcode, no time
damn! I've left them at home.
We're not that sure
what a good time will be,
by Newton's logic it'll be slow
given the lack of gravity.
A stunning earth selfie
elation on landing
then the disappointment
last minute cancellation!

2. HUNSTANTON PROMENADE

Run Report: Looking for Linda, 14/03/2020

On the drive from my east coast hometown of Great Yarmouth to Hunstanton you realise just how large Norfolk is. From the Acle Straight and its desolate marshes to the beautiful village of Guist with its clock tower, the journey has many rewards for the early riser. On the promenade it wasn't a case of Sunny Hunny as grey cloud, drizzle and a strong breeze reminded all that it was still early spring. Thankful to be running in light of the ongoing Coronavirus pandemic, 88 people turned up to participate in Hunstanton Promenade's 23rd event. Run director John Crowley commendably got us underway quickly after a briefing in which Linda from Watford's birthday (more on this later) was announced along with Emily Crown's 50th run (which she celebrated with a new pb of 25:32). Visitors came from as far afield as the Middle East and Barking.

And so we were off along a slippery promenade, periodically sprayed by waves crashing into the concrete seawall. The Wash was resplendent in its melancholic vastness. Heads down, the journey south took us past the Sea Life Centre and deserted fun fair (with a bizarre Dracula ride) to the turning point on the precipitous Hunstanton Hump, itself a slipway! Relieved to have a tailwind, it was great sharing a word or two with the fabulous marshals (20 terrific volunteers this morning), even receiving some lovely feedback on my run reports from a runner, thank you all! A second out and back lap led to the finish funnel; exhausted but pleased to have run in the circumstances. Renegade Runner Charlotte Dixon defied the wind to record an overall parkrun pb of 27:38.

The post run drinks were shared in the Sailing Club, free from the bracingly cold breeze which dogged us. A total of 29 runners beat the poet (26:56), the scribbler struggling with the gusty breeze off The Wash! Those in front were Thetford AC's Andy Fleet who ran a new overall parkrun pb (22:16)! Andy paced me to a parkrun pb at Thetford last year, so I was pleased to see him achieve his.

In this remote corner of The Wash, whose name derives from the old English word for mud, slime and ooze, are wonderful cliffs with a seam of red chalk. The cliffs are just a short walk from the finish and a must see before you leave Hunstanton.

Poetry Corner

After the run, I caught up with Linda and her husband David in the Sailing Club. Our discourse pogoed from punk to the seawalls and sandbanks of The Wash. I was interested to learn that the Romans built seawall embankments to protect land from flooding, giving the area a long history of human colonisation. So inspired to have met some genuine folk, I've written a short poem about our lengthy chat:

Rumours

>the Pistols
>on a Yarmouth juke box
>in Seventy-seven
>enough to drive you
>to Fleetwood Mac

> you saw the isolation
> in post-punk eyes
> joy unleashed
> by the loneliness
> of The Wash

As the team of volunteers departed, I was informed that I was talking to Linda from Barking, not Linda Hallahan from Watford with the aforementioned birthday! Amid the confusion, I had made friends with Linda and David Weaver, Barking parkrunners on tour! Musing on an interesting morning, I will definitely be back to run the summer route which takes athletes up the cliffs to the lighthouse.

This was my last parkrun before COVID-19 parkrun cessation.

Don't say you weren't warned at Ganavan Sands!

3. GANAVAN SANDS

Run Report: Skyfall (avoided), 21/08/2021

After an absence of eight years I returned to Scotland, this time with my 11-year-old son, Joseph. The trip to the West Highlands saw us drive through the desolate Rannoch Moor, before the breathtakingly bleak Glencoe. A quick stop at the famous Glen Etive road featured in Skyfall was obligatory for a couple of Bond fans! A few days in Fort William involved an ascent of Ben Nevis. Big Ben was a tough walk, but the success of the summit is something neither of us will forget, with its precipitous north face and observatory ruin. It wasn't ideal preparation for a parkrun, but it's such a long way to travel from the south that we fell into the trap of trying to squeeze too much in. This also my first parkrun as a runner since the resumption of parkrun in July 2021 after the COVID-19 cessation which lasted 16 long months.

With spirits high, we arrived at Ganavan Sands for our first Scottish parkrun. I was excited for the varied course, and the panoramic views across to Mull. The Bay is known for its underwater meadows of seagrass, which provide vital habitat for seahorses and eels. A sign by the start gate described the infamous and unsolved Appin Murder of 1752 which followed the Jacobite uprising and defeat at Culloden in 1746. A second sign informed us 'route ahead contains steep gradients.' My son foolishly ignored it and sprinted up the hill at the start! Apparently, his calf muscles felt like they'd been shredded on the second hill!

This week we saw 100 people running, jogging and walking the hallowed 3.1 miles which was higher than the previous week and the second highest attendance behind 104 in 2017. We had a good array of athletes from far and wide (well, places such as Essex, Somerset and North Wales), 37 first-timers (and Superman) and 13 fantastic volunteers including run director Doreen. There were some fine times from the front runners, including first finishers Raymond Hughes (18:48) and Cara Bradley (23:12). Luckily, we got the parkrun in before the sky fell and the rain descended. My short poetic musing from Room 101 of an M6 Travelodge is:

Flyfall

midge

with an interest

in stride length

still at large

on the moor

cadence

when the sky

falls

Poetry Corner

As wonderful as dead Scottish poets are, I'm so pleased to present a fine living one in this poetry corner. Poet and songwriter Ellen McAteer is a Thames born, Clyde built writer with her poetry firmly rooted in the culture and heritage of Scotland. She currently edits the prestigious Poetry London magazine, founded a Glasgow bookshop, and ran the Aldeburgh Festival in Suffolk for The Poetry Trust. The following poem by Ellen, appropriate for today's setting, was first published in Aesthetica, Issue 13.

Mountain Song

We did not climb the mountain.
While the sun shone
I wanted you to see
What was important to me:
A riot of blue stars in spiked grass
The frowning sand, fat gold rolls of it
The water that showed us, clear as glass
Toes among stones
But was dark as cut agate
Where the waves sliced it.
And you saw. You understood.
Like the good
Man I knew you to be:
You walked on the edge of my world
And did not step on a flower,
Or laugh at a rock
(The sea-cut granite, fallen from the head of the cliff
Like a ponderous thought).
And while the mountain that was you
With your 360 degree view
Stood on the edge of my mind
Like a reproach –
I made you walk by the sea,
Made you walk in the valley of me.
And now I pray for another sunny day –
But the mountain stands shrouded, clouded, grey.

4. CHILTON FIELDS

Run Report: Teenage kicks (so hard to beat), 11/09/2021

As a parkrun tourist, the new run at Chilton Fields (Stowmarket) meant that I needed to visit it to complete all 12 Suffolk events (challenge known as Suff-ok). The town has a connection with legendary radio DJ John Peel, who lived nearby. I'd been to gigs at the John Peel Centre and performed at the Suffolk Poetry Festival there. So with spirits high, I was looking forward to a new parkrun location.

The run is a three-lap course, generally flat and on grass and cinder track (average run time 29:31). No dogs are allowed. Each lap starts on the playing fields heading north. Runners then turn onto a surfaced path along the edge of a housing development (the track is narrow though), circuit an arable field, briefly take in the Paupers' Graves (more on that later) before running along a green lane back to the sports field. The parkrun is a welcome addition to the Suffolk events, presenting another off-road run for those who prefer a soft surface underfoot. Marshals were plentiful and cheerful in their encouragement. I think Chilton Fields will go from strength to strength providing parkrunning for locals and bring tourists to Suffolk.

The total of 114 finishers was the highest Chilton Fields attendance so far, with five athletes (if you have an athlete number, you're an athlete!) new to parkrun. Scott Williams (17:30, new PB) and Sophie Carter (23:06) excelled as first finishers while the John Peel Teenage Kicks award goes to Luke Heather (19:16) who achieved a new PB for the JM15-17 age class. He'll be so hard to beat! This week, 76 athletes beat the poet (31:28), a sorry state of affairs for the waffling wordsmith on return from injury.

Poetry Corner

After the parkrun, I explored the Paupers' Graves in the south-west corner of the site. I didn't notice the brown sign to the Graves on the run but they're easy to find after you've finished. At the entrance was a large (around 8 cm long) elephant hawk-moth caterpillar. Moving it safely to the long grass away from trampling feet, I entered the cemetery. The graveyard was formerly overgrown with brambles but has been cleared and is now managed as a conservation area for wildlife with selective grass cutting and trees planted. The paupers' graves were associated with a workhouse which opened in 1798. Many of the workhouse residents were buried in the graveyard, some after dying from smallpox. The paupers were buried in shallow graves with a simple wooden cross. Each cross had a metal plate with a number on it but no name. Many crosses have been refound during vegetation clearance and can be seen. The site is reported to have a floating apparition and nearby, fairies are said to have helped a ploughman with his lunch! How many parkruns can boast this?! Finishing with the artistic portion of the report, here's a short poem about the Paupers' Graves:

no trace

of the workhouse

a pauper's cross

more than

just a number

The Paupers' Graves at Chilton Fields

5. SEWERBY

Run Report: Every step you take, 25/09/2021

I returned to Yorkshire after running York parkrun on 1st February 2020, the weekend of the COVID-19 outbreak in the city. It was good to be back in the north, this time on the coast. I was tempted by the spectacular views of Bridlington Bay from Sewerby parkrun and the varied route of the course which included steps. Sadly, I'm no stranger to steps, having run the Lowestoft Scores route in Suffolk (401 steps over 4.75 miles), Whitby's 199 steps to the Abbey (minus goth attire) and Newark parkrun which has the stairway to Devon (and Sconce Park). Having picked up a knee injury during the first lockdown, it was with some trepidation that I looked forward to Sewerby parkrun.

A Robin Hood's Bay sunrise percolating through cottage windows was the perfect start to the morning. Arriving at Sewerby Hall after an hour's drive, I soaked up the friendly pre-run atmosphere. At the start line, a fenced enclosure had deer among the long grass, something you don't see at many parkruns. The first mile provided panoramic views of Bridlington Bay as the surfaced path swept downhill to the turnaround. I was lulled into a false sense of security by the gentle topography of the start. The second mile was mostly uphill along the cliff edge path, admiring the stunning chalk cliffs stretching into the distance between breaths! For me, the long uphill slog was the hardest part of the course as forewarned by numerous marshals before the off.

Turning into Sewerby Hall, the final mile is a meandering route through the gardens and woodland to the staircase of sorrow. Every move you make. Every step you take. They'll provide that final drop-kick to the energy levels. One step beyond, the finish funnel was hidden from view in the winding labyrinth of the gardens, signs helpfully pointed out where there were 400 and 200 metres to go. After a post-parkrun drink at the charming Clock Tower Café (a must-do), the parkrun fresh feeling was neutralised by a bracing dip in the sea (there are steps down the cliffs to the sandy beach). To summarise, the varied course has it all for the runner and walker: uphill sections (elevation gain around 150 ft.), surfaced paths, off-road sections and lots of twists and turns. You really have no idea where you're going to finish until you reach the picturesque finishing straight lined with statues in front of the Georgian country house.

Event 442 had 245 finishers and was made possible by 24 fantastic volunteers. A special shout out to timekeeper Jayne Sissons who has volunteered over 400 times; an incredible contribution to Sewerby parkrun. She was joined in the volunteering by Josh Smith (With Me Now club), touring with Lauren Turner who ran well (24:39). First finishers were the greyhounds Liam Morris (18:00) and Emma Artley (23:11). Christopher Humphries ran his 50th parkrun and is eligible for the red t-shirt, congratulations to him on reaching this first significant milestone. Six people ran their first parkrun and hopefully began their long running adventure: Joanne Deighton, Chloe Harrison, Jo Hodgson, Madeline Rowntree, Sarah Smith and Sarah Newman. It's fair to say, many of us would not have started running without the incentive of parkrun. A total of 136 athletes beat the poet (31:11), not too difficult an achievement these days.

Poetry Corner

Finishing with the artistic portion of the report, here's a haiku-like poem to celebrate Sewerby parkrun:

step by step
a runner's shadow

steals
from the lungs
to give to the heart

Running along the top of the cliffs at Sewerby

6. SANDRINGHAM

Run Report: Another run bites the dust, 09/10/2021

It was an early start for the journey from Gorleston (east Norfolk) to Sandringham. The drive was accompanied by lingering mist over Breydon Marshes and along the A47 on the first cool morning of autumn, or so it seemed. I'd been reading about a knitted Sandringham House the night before in the local paper so all roads were pointing to the Queen's much-loved retreat. On arrival at Sandringham the sun was rising above the trees, the mist starting to lift. I could immediately see that this was a special parkrun venue in idyllic grounds with woodland and scenic views. The new event was made possible by the dedication of the event team and parkrun ambassador, Bridget Plowright, who has been involved with establishing several Norfolk parkruns including Hunstanton. Today's run director, Lucinda White, who works for the Sandringham Estate, did a sterling job to make sure proceedings passed smoothly including processing of the results in the café afterwards. Several of the volunteers work for the Estate and have been instrumental in bringing the parkrun to life.

The run itself is an extremely attractive two-lap route through the woods of the Sandringham Estate starting near the children's playground. Here, the Queen's bee meadow was still flowering with vivid blue cornflowers and orange poppies, providing a late season source of pollen and nectar for pollinators. Don't be fooled by the fast start to the run which takes you past the playground where an old water tower has been converted into a tree house slide. A slight downhill slope makes it easy to get carried away with the early pace along Princess's Drive (part of the aptly named Scenic Drive) winding underneath a layered canopy of deciduous (beech, oak and sweet chestnut) and coniferous trees such as Corsican pine. Part of the run passes very close to Wild Wood, just a small part of the 280 hectares of the Royal Park Wood and the 1400 hectares of woodland at Sandringham. The route then opens up to a wide grassy ride which provides views to the east, mist permitting! Cutting across this grassy strip the run is soon back under the trees of the Scotch Belt until it opens up again near the end of the first lap and finish funnel. The route is mainly off-road although there is a short section of surfaced path along Princess's Drive. The gentle undulations can catch you out particularly if you've run too quickly on the first lap, so good pacing is needed here, something I've not mastered after nearly 100 parkruns!

Event 4 had 149 finishers and was made possible by 18 fantastic volunteers. First finishers were Daniel Smith (18:24, new PB for his 100th parkrun) and Bethan Everson (19:34). Franklyn Richards ran his 50th parkrun and is eligible for the red t-shirt, congratulations to him on reaching this first significant milestone. Twenty people ran their first parkrun and hopefully began their long running adventure, while several running clubs were in evidence including the Great Yarmouth Road Runners, Lynnsport Ladybirds, Peterborough Paws Canicross and Renegade Runners. A total of 108 athletes beat the poet (32:46), the wordsmith waning badly after the first mile. I've struggled to get back the fitness or mental resilience required to run sub-30 minute parkruns. I spoke to several runners afterwards who feel the same way; the lockdowns had hit them hard too. The key is to persist, keep training and turning up, the worm will turn one day. I've missed the social aspect of parkrun more than the running to be honest! The chance to tour as the parkrun poet and meet new people in fantastic settings like the Sandringham Estate is what motivates me.

Poetry Corner

Finishing with the artistic portion of the report, here's a haiku-like poem for the natural beauty of the parkrun:

the buzz

of wild wood

start line

cornflowers

unnoticed in mist

Misty morning at Sandringham

7. HARLESTON MAGPIES

Run Report: Morning, Mr. Magpie, 23/10/2021

The journey began early for the hour's drive from Manningtree in Essex to Harleston for the new parkrun's fifth event. On the A140, the Magpie at Little Stonham was sadly without the wooden pub sign straddling the road after it was struck by a vehicle in July 2021. Apparently, the original sign was used as a gibbet for hanging highwaymen so has historical significance and should be replaced. Arriving at Harleston Magpies Hockey Club, there was enough time for a warm up jog and chat with the run director Don Bennett, before we were off on time.

The run is a three-lap affair, each lap taking you on a winding route around two grass playing fields which skirt hedgerows and woodland. In each field you venture into the middle via a coat hanger-shaped loop which is well marshalled and sign-posted. The route is entirely off-road on grass so there may be cuttings which could slow you down a little due to the thatch. There is a short, gentle slope to negotiate at the end of each lap but the Harleston Hump shouldn't worry anyone too much. Interestingly, there was a giant puffball mushroom along one of the hedgerow boundaries which somehow avoided being trampled during the run. The large white, football-sized fungus is a familiar sight of autumn. The marshals throughout were friendly and encouraging, I sure as hell needed it when puffing along like a steam train! There was free tea and coffee afterwards which was pleasant, with a donation to the hockey club welcomed.

The hockey club was formed in 1935 and is one of the premier hockey clubs in East Anglia. Apparently, the magpie in the hockey club title is a reference to a local pub of the same name.

The hockey club balcony provides a view of the undulating farmland of the picturesque Waveney Valley, but unfortunately there were no magpies to salute to fend off bad luck! The grass fields are fringed with hedgerows and woodland with a gravel pit (the whole area is part of Shotford Heath) which look like havens for wildlife. The grass fields we run on are probably filled-in gravel pits. The Suffolk Heritage Explorer shows that in the 1970s a small pointed hand axe and fossilised remains of mammoth, rhinoceros, auroch, bison and horse were found on Shotford Heath. A ring ditch, probably the remains of a Bronze Age barrow or burial mound, can be seen as a cropmark on aerial photographs of the area. As my son always says, my run reports have nothing to do with running so we must return to the events of Saturday morning.

Event 5 had 66 finishers and was made possible by 20 fantastic volunteers including one of the fastest tail-walkers I've come across in Robin Anthony Farrar (44:41). First finishers were Andrew Farn (18:52) and Madeleine Tatham (22:45, a new female course record). Congratulations to Jo Hodgson for running the 3.1 miles without stopping for the first time. Several running clubs were in evidence including the Beccles and Bungay Harriers, Bungay Black Dog RC, Dereham Runners AC (on tour), Lowestoft Road Runners and Worlingham RoadRunnerz. A total of 40 athletes beat the poet (30:24), the waning wordsmith wandering lonely as a magpie. I'm just starting to get back into parkrun after a lockdown knee injury and COVID lethargy. I didn't realise just how hard it would be with the fitness returning slower than expected. My impatience to return to the 'pace' of old has been tempered by what my body is able to do and I'll never take a sub-30 parkrun for granted again. A new book details how runners, including Lingwood's Phil Henry, coped with running during the lockdowns. The book is titled 'A Tussle of Clouds' and is edited by top fenland runner and poet,

Elisabeth Sennitt-Clough and me. The book was published on 29 October by Stour Valley Publishing.

After the parkrun, a trip into town was rewarded with the rustic clock-tower dominated high street and its Georgian architecture. Bacon bap consumed, there was a short trip to Mendham to take photographs of the Sir Alfred Munnings Hotel. Munnings was a famous painter of horses and landscapes born in Mendham Mill, who is of particular interest to me through my work with the Munnings Museum in Dedham (Essex) as a poet.

Poetry Corner

Finishing with the artistic portion of the report, here's a fungus and magpie inspired haiku-like poem:

>morning dew
>I slip by the puffball

>you had
>to be there
>magpie

8. SHORNE WOODS

Run Report: Traveller's Joy, 06/11/2021

The hedgerows in the North Downs Area of Outstanding Natural Beauty (AONB) were wreathed in the wild climbing plant Traveller's Joy, known in historic times as Old Man's Beard due to the fluffy seed heads seen in late summer and autumn. The plant is frequent on the chalky soils of the North Downs on which Shorne Woods parkrun takes place. The hilly nature of the Downs is evident at Shorne Woods where the parkrun course undulates through woodland, twisting and turning past ponds dug for clay. The site was part of the medieval Cobham Hall Estate, the ancient coppice woods full of bluebells in spring. The woods have a wide range of trees such as hornbeam, oak, sweet chestnut and yew and are superb for fungi.

Shorne Woods is reportedly flat but I'd describe the route as undulating due to the 100+ ft. elevation gain on the completion of the three laps. For my 100th parkrun, I wanted a picturesque venue and Shorne Woods delivered on that magnificently and it's only right and proper to run up slopes on the Downs. The run comprises three laps, each lap taking you on a winding route around the woodland with several slopes which appear innocuous at first but by the final lap test legs and lungs. I enjoy trail runs more than tarmac ones; running between the trees with the yellow, brown and red colours of autumn leaves was worth the trip and exertion. I managed to miss a giant sculpted great crested newt by the edge of the path but did find the green man in the sensory garden afterwards and a wooden dragonfly on the pond behind the visitor centre.

Event 378 had 238 finishers and was made possible by 17 fantastic volunteers. Lesley Covington completed her 25th

parkrun to earn her first running vest, while David White joined the 50 Club. Polly Akehurst (JW15-17) completed her 10th run to enter the Junior 10 club. Congratulations to all runners for achieving these important milestones. There were 8 athletes new to parkrun and 28 people recorded a course PB. First finishers were John Whittaker (18:50) and Hannah Mitchell (21:04). A total of 140 athletes beat the poet (31:44), the scribbler suffering on the slopes. Having struggled on the return to parkrun after lockdowns and a knee injury, I've talked to many runners and walkers who are finding the return to action physically and mentally strenuous.

Poetry Corner

Finishing with the artistic portion of the report, here's a haiku-like poem for the wild heart of Shorne Woods parkrun:

good for age
old man's beard

if anywhere's home
why not here
green man

9. SWANSEA BAY

Run Report: Singing in our pains, 20/11/2021

The trip to Swansea was part of a long weekend catching up with friends exploring the Gower Peninsula. For me it was also a pilgrimage to discover the birthplace of the legendary poet, Dylan Thomas. Thomas was born in 5 Cwmdonkin Drive in the appropriately named Uplands area of Swansea in 1914. He became widely popular as a poet until his untimely death in New York on 9th November 1953 at the age of just 39. He composed some of the finest lyrical poems of the 20th century including Do Not Go Gentle Into That Good Night and Fern Hill. The title of this report refers to the famous poem Fern hill which closes "though I sang in my chains, like the sea." Given how hard it has been to return to parkrun due to the loss of fitness, it feels like I'm singing in chains these days along with quite a few others!

Fortunately for me, Swansea Bay is a flat and fast course starting at the Cenotaph. The views across Swansea Bay sands are majestic, the course following the arc of the shoreline heading towards the Mumbles. We ran past Swansea University in the outward half, shortly followed by Swansea Footgolf before looping back near Blackpill Lido to begin the final push to the finish where refreshments can be obtained at the Secret Beach Bar and Kitchen. The course records tell an incredible story with Kristian Jones running 14:27 in December 2017, one of the fastest parkrun times while Elinor Kirk excelled with 16:33 for the fastest female time along the promenade. I'm content to tour around the UK experiencing the best parkruns out there. It was my second time in Wales, having run Severn Bridge just before lockdown in 2020. One of my first parkruns since restart was the hilly Ganavan Sands on the west coast of Scotland, something akin to Cwmdonkin Drive in steepness. I'm unsure what completing the challenge of running a parkrun in England, Scotland and Wales is called. I suggest Try Nations or Great Britran!

Event 233 had 367 finishers and was made possible by 22 fantastic volunteers. Five people (Mark Andrews, Steve Bevan, Luke Davies, Janet Hargreaves and Royston Whitehouse) completed their 25th parkrun to earn their first running vest, while Tenniel O'Brien and Jackie Meyrick joined the 50 Club. Elizabeth Barclay completed her 100th run with a balloon. Congratulations to all runners for achieving these important milestones. There were 18 athletes new to parkrun including my friends Nick Harpur (29:52) and Julie Cooley (36:29) on her birthday. First finishers were Geraint Williams (16:50) and Graciela Diaz (21:11). A total of 257 athletes beat the poet (29:56), the writer raging against the dying of the light on the return leg.

Poetry Corner

A poetry corner for Swansea Bay parkrun cannot be written without mention of my good friend, the poet Ian Griffiths. Ian was born in Swansea and explored the Gower Peninsula as a boy. His love of Dylan Thomas stemmed from childhood, leading him into poetry and a meeting with Lenin's bodyguard in Russia many years ago. Ian performed his Dylan tribute show 'Singing in my Chains' throughout the UK and on Long Island in New York. A fine lyrical poet in his own right, he continues to find inspiration from the coastal setting of the Stour Estuary in Suffolk. His 2018 poem Hide and Seek has lines in it which could easily relate to a Swansea Bay parkrun in spring:

A Wren had made its nest
Safe within her moss cocoon
With pounding heart
She hears my step approach
Feels my shadow pass.

Finishing with the artistic portion of the report, here's my haiku-like poem inspired by Swansea Bay parkrun and Dylan Thomas:

by fern hill
sand gathers

morning stars
between them
it's all possible

under
the cover
of daylight

no-one notices
the moon steal away

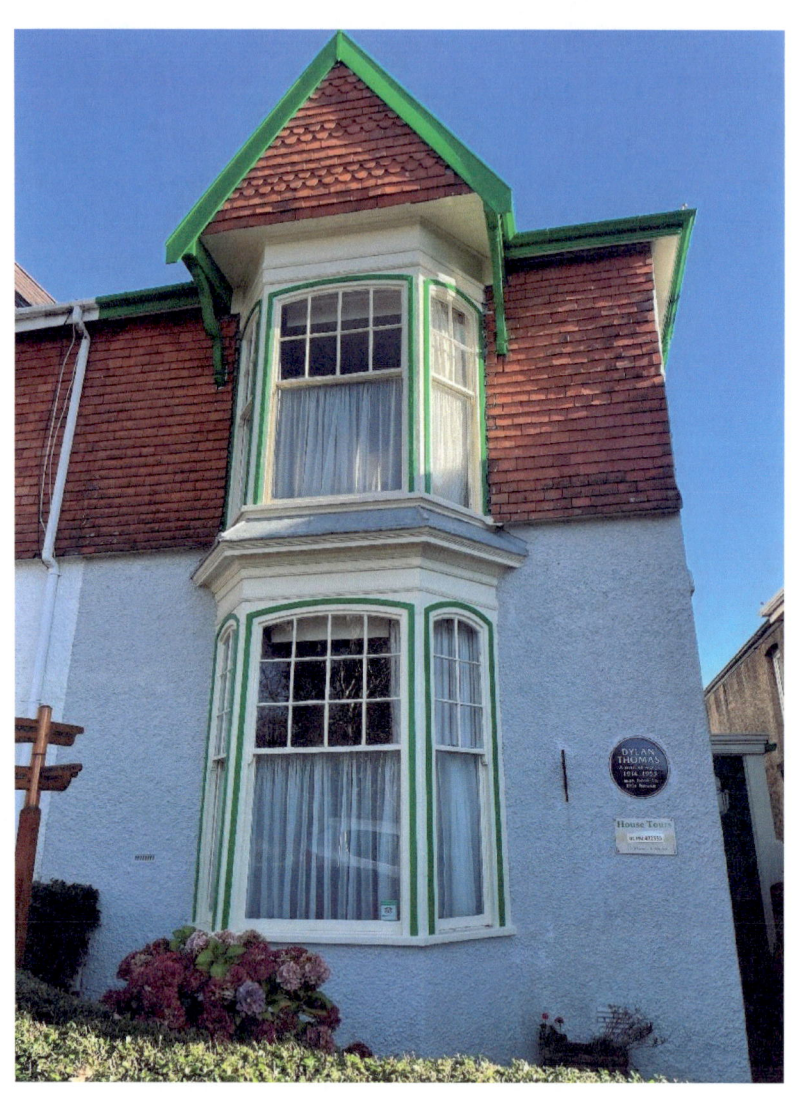

The birthplace of Swansea poet, Dylan Thomas

10. MARKSHALL ESTATE

Event run 27/11/2021

Parkrun started at Markshall Estate near Coggeshall in north Essex on 13th November 2021. I stayed away from the inaugural to avoid adding to the numbers but visited on their third event with my son, Joseph. The Estate is a beautiful location for a parkrun. The course took us through woodland, past meadows and up one or two slopes to provide a varied parkrunning experience. I struggled on the steep slope halfway through, fortunately you only have to run it once! The long downhill section to the finish is an enjoyable leg stretcher to earn some of the time back lost on the hill.

Formerly the site of a Jacobean country house demolished in 1950, the estate is now a well-known arboretum with gardens. There are over 5000 trees from every temperate area and one of the most intimate walled gardens around. Plenty of scope for post-parkrun adventures here.

a voice

from the past

overtakes me

11. MARKET RASEN RACECOURSE

Run Report: Saturday light's alright for running!
04/12/2021

Coming up from Great Yarmouth like an unwanted weather front, I visited Somersby on parkrun eve. The village was the birthplace of the famous poet, Alfred, Lord Tennyson, in 1809. Tennyson's poignant words from the poem Ulysses could easily apply to the ethos of parkrun:

> One equal temper of heroic hearts,
> Made weak by time and fate, but strong in will
> To strive, to seek, to find, and not to yield.

Tennyson wrote several poems about his native Lincolnshire and local nature. In The Lady of Shalott, Tennyson used the term 'Wold' as a Lincolnshire phrase for hill. The Wolds has the highest ground (highest point 168 m, 551 ft.) between Yorkshire and Kent in eastern England and is designated as an Area of Outstanding Natural Beauty (AONB). Market Rasen Racecourse is located on the western edge of the Wolds. The name of the town means 'place (market) at the planks' in old English, presumably referring to a plank bridge across the river. Charles Dickens once called it the sleepiest town in England!

The title of this report refers to a song written by famous Market Rasen lyricist, Bernie Taupin. Taupin spent his teenage years in the town before going on to write some of Elton John's most well-known songs such as Saturday Night's Alright for Fighting which was reputably inspired by punch-ups in a local pub. I had other song titles up my sleeve for the run report: Candles in the

Wind (if stormy), Goodbye Yellow Quick Road (if not windy), Rocket Man, We're Still Standing and of course, Tiny Scanner (okay, I'll stop here!). Before I lose the plot further, back to Market Rasen Racecourse which was founded in 1924.

Market Rasen Racecourse is a mostly flat and fast two and a half lap parkrun taking you around the inside of the National Hunt course with jumps and water features (thankfully not for runners or walkers!). The racecourse environment is far from featureless with grandstand, bushes, flood reservoirs, fringing forest and a panoramic view of the Wolds. But like York, the open nature of the racecourse means that it can be windy. Fortunately, it was only breezy on my visit and the snow that fell in previous days had melted. The run is mostly on tarmac, ideal for quick times. Along the back straight at the start of each lap, there is a slight incline (the Rasen Ridge!) which you'll feel a little but after that around the far bend it's downhill so you can open the stride and make the time back. The course is comprised of a small lap (1 k) and two complete circuits of the racecourse (2 k each) which is quite handy for pacing.

Event 80 had 78 finishers and was made possible by 15 fantastic volunteers. A big thank you to Mike Wells who completed his 100th volunteering stint at parkrun and Sarah Wells for taking the gorgeous Sprocker Spaniel Millie for her first tail walk. Raymond Clayton completed his 25th parkrun to earn the first milestone running vest while Martin Arthur finished his first run in a very impressive 22:13, hopefully starting a long and rewarding parkrun journey. First finishers were Lincoln speedster Raymond Clayton (18:31) and the sprightly Deborah Simpson (23:01), well done to them. A total of 45 athletes beat the poet (29:49), the writer made weak by time and fate! This was only my third sub-30 parkrun since the post-COVID restart. I have Hannah Beckett (with hound) and Nick Waltz to thank as they spurred me on at the two mile mark. In the end, we all dipped under 30 minutes proving that teamwork gets results. This is what I love about parkrun, the collective support.

Tim's Tourist Tip-off – Walesby Ramblers' Church

In an all new section of my reports and mainly for parkrun tourist John Buchanan, here's my top place to visit if you're making a weekend of it. All Saints Church in Walesby (short drive from Market Rasen) affords spectacular views of the racecourse from the hilltop along with Lincoln Cathedral on a clear day. The church and associated hill walk (100 ft. ascent) has much to enjoy even in winter. All Saints Church became a pilgrimage for ramblers in the 1930s and for this reason it is often referred to as the Ramblers' Church. There is even a stained glass window dedicated to them. The churchyard is managed for wildlife in conjunction with advice from conservation charity Caring for God's Acre to maintain the wildflower (e.g. Bluebell, Knapweed and Star-of-Bethlehem), insect (bees and butterflies) and mammal populations. I saw a herd of red deer close up in an adjacent field on the Viking Way. For the budding Indiana Jones there is a probable Roman villa nearby too. Go check it out!

Poetry Corner

A poetry corner for a racecourse would not be complete without a fine equine poem by Jane Lovell that has a hint of parkrun galloping to it. Jane also had a poem in my York parkrun report just before COVID hit, so the circle is now complete. Enjoy!

Meath Street Horses

we ride them hard, these gypsy mares
high as cowboys
yipping up the tired air, the tired light
pools of glimming oil shattered by hooves

cracking past streets of boarded up lives
candy-black graffiti, roaming feral dogs
the old years hanging in doorways
all blown smoke and narrowed eyes

we know the score
catch us hard-arsing it past St Catherine's
her plumes of flame and bright glass cracking
the font shizzy with smashed ice

we are kings of the backstreets: the piebald,
the proud, eyes fixed the long o' the street
that window to a tiny sky, the moment wound
tight round our bitten hands

them and us, we're brazen as hell
we don't know
we never seen what's beyond

I finish with a haiku-like poem inspired by my first visit to Market Rasen and the Wolds.

late night
someone misses
the Wolds view

The Lincolnshire Wolds as a backdrop for parkrun

12. MANOR FIELD, WHITTLESEY

Run Report: Fairytale of Dew Park, 18/12/2021

'twas the run before Christmas, when all through the fen

not a gadget was stirring, not even a Garmin

the stockings were worn by parkrunners with care

in hopes that St. Nicholas soon would bring beer

Modified lines from the classic Clement Clarke Moore poem inspired by run director Erica Cave's sung briefing for the Christmas parkrun!

The fens area has one big advantage for unfit runners: it's flat. For me, it was also an excuse to meet up with poetic running friend Elisabeth Sennitt Clough, who is the chief mover and shaker in the fenland poetry community. It was Lightning Liz who invited me to Manor Field for the run. Three other members from the Clough crew (Rebekah, Sarah and Tim) were present making it a family affair.

I've only run one fenland parkrun at the intimate and friendly Littleport near Ely. The majestic Ely cathedral, known as the 'Ship of the Fens' dominated the eyeline like a gothic colossus on my drive to Littleport. This morning was an early start (6 am), traveling up from Essex with the depressing drizzle, bypassing Ely Cathedral on the mundane A14 corridor, to reach Whittlesey between Peterborough and March. The name is derived from old English, maybe from Witles ieg, which means "Witel's island" with "Witel" being the name of an unknown man. The island of Whittlesey would have been high and dry ground in the otherwise drained fens. These days parts of the town are around 10 m above sea level which is almost mountainous for fenland!

The parkrun itself is flat and on grass comprising one small lap and three loops around the boundary of Manor Park. There's an attractive stretch along the original course of the River Nene (Briggate River) taking in Ashline Lock although it was muddy and quite slippery. At the end of the river section, we turned right through a short but pleasant wooded section before a course diversion took us along two short sections of hard surfaced path (sprint!!!) and a small hump (the Manor Mound) which felt like a mountain on the third lap! I found myself covered in a fine mist of dew and sweat when I finally finished. The cool and drizzly morning was perfect for running with hardly any wind at all although I regret arriving too late to warm up as my calf muscles ached for most of the afternoon.

Event 104 had 78 finishers and was made possible by 23 fantastic volunteers. Ethan Locke (JM11-14) ran an incredible 20:53 (73% age grade) to join the Junior 10 Club and earn his first milestone vest. Angela King completed her 50th parkrun to earn the coveted claret milestone vest. Well done to both runners. First finishers were Kirk Brawn (18:17) and Elisabeth Sennitt-Clough (21:54) who adopted her effective grass running technique, well done to them both. A total of 43 athletes beat the poet (29:33), the scribbler slipping and sliding around the course! And finally, a special mention to all those wearing fancy dress including a reindeer, several santas and the elf-assisted turkey who ran impressively despite the restrictions of the outfit!

Tim's Tourist Tip-off – Festival of the Straw Bear

Apart from Christmas, the best time to visit Whittlesey for parkrun tourism would be to coincide with the Festival of the Straw Bear which originally took place on Plough Tuesday in January (first Tuesday after Twelfth Night) every year. On this weekend, a man or boy was covered in straw and would pass from house to house where he danced for beer, food or money. The original festival died out in 1909 as it was seen as begging, but it was revived in 1980 and is now staged on the second weekend in January. The Straw Bear is accompanied along the streets by its keeper and a whole menagerie including clog dancers, rappers and morris men and women. At the end of the weekend, the bear costume is burned.

Poetry Corner

I finish with a haiku-like renku (verses linked) poem inspired by Whittlesey, co-written with Elisabeth Sennitt-Clough (italics) which references the fens in several ways including the straw bear and the mysterious fen tiger. The wild fen tiger has been spotted all over the fens and Cambridgeshire including at Coldham's Common parkrun (not during the run I should add!) and Whittlesey.

A Renku for Whittlesey Parkrun

a thick coat

of straw

for the bear

as it passes

from house to house

lustrous black coat
for the beast
they call the fen tiger

old shuck
needs a new trick

our last days
strangely lit
by red eyes

where are the stars
you spoke of

dark soil glints
with constellations:
half-sunken farms

a hill, in the fens
you've got to be joking

13. FERRY MEADOWS

Run Report: Battle Wrapping, 25/12/2021

Christmas Day. Six am. No sign of Santa. After a quick Weetabix, I'm off to Ferry Meadows, Peterborough, for the parkrun. I usually run in the massive peloton at Norwich on the big day but this year a journey from Essex was part of my drive home to Gorleston, Norfolk. Pootling along the necessary roads, the hour was darkest before the dawn with cold wind and rain all the way and an eerily deserted Cambridge Services on the A14. As part of my parkrun superstition commenced at Harleston Magpies earlier in the year, I saluted each and every magpie for good luck!

I was not disappointed with Ferry Meadows in Nene Park. Ferry Meadows is located beside the River Nene and is a significant recreational area in Peterborough. Ferry Meadows biggest claim to fame was featuring in the James Bond films, GoldenEye and Octopussy. In Goldeneye (1995), Ferry Meadows Station on the Nene Valley Railway appeared briefly in the scenes with the armour-plated Russian train and was cited as an exotic location for Roger Moore's Bond in Octopussy (1983)! Originally, there was to be a mock-up of the Berlin Wall in Ferry Meadows but the Nene Valley Railway was eventually used for the scenes involving the circus train in Octopussy. Curiously, there are 15 registered parkrunners named James Bond! To my knowledge, no Bonds have run or walked Ferry Meadows, shaken or stirred!

The parkrun course itself is an all-tarmac affair starting at Ferry Meadows Café before circuiting Lynch Lake and passing over Ham Bridge, finally looping around a wooded area and heading back to the start location. Runners cross Ham Bridge again and finish at Roman Point, which was apparently an ancient military settlement. The bridge feels like Everest on the last leg of the run while the slightly uphill finish will test your sprinting skill! I enjoyed the route immensely while the support from marshals and other runners/walkers was incredible.

Event 372 had 412 finishers and was made possible by 35 fantastic volunteers. Adrian Ash, Sharon Ash, Jean Hobday and David Towns joined the 100 parkrun club to earn the black milestone running vest. Ray Causten, Caroline Garner, Claire Holden and Jayne Pell all completed their 50th parkrun to earn the coveted red t-shirt. The 25 club has five new members: Simon Barrett, Jack Bone, David Thorold, Duncan Vessey and Elliott Wilson. Congratulations to all and to the 23 athletes who recorded new course PBs. For Christmas morning we had plenty of fancy dress on show, my favourite was the guy with a turkey on his head! A mother and baby also finished, a joyous sight as the youngster was clearly enjoying the parkrun. There were plenty of walkers in attendance, encouraging to see.

First finishers were the supremely quick Ewan Davidson (16:12) and Jess Varley (19:45), well done to them both for recording excellent times despite the cold, wet and breezy weather. A total of 251 athletes beat the poet (30:08), the scribbler slowly skipping around the course like Santa after a night on the sherry, losing crucial seconds tying up an errant lace (thanks to all who alerted me!)

Tim's Tourist Tip-off - John Clare's Cottage

My top place to visit if you're making a weekend of it in 2022, is the poet John Clare's Cottage in nearby Helpston. Clare, one of England's greatest poets, was born in 1793 next to the Bluebell public house, the son of a farm labourer. The lane, said to be haunted by ghosts and goblins in those days, is a peaceful retreat now, the cottage's white walls topped with a thatch roof. A statue of Clare can be seen in the courtyard. Clare's poetry was concerned with rural issues until he was admitted to an asylum in later life, dying in 1864. The lines from his poem 'Emmonsail's Heath in Winter' could easily apply to a bleak midwinter parkrun at Ferry Meadows: While the old heron from the lonely lake, starts slow and flaps its melancholy wing...

Poetry Corner

I first met Mark Grist in 2016 at the Woodbridge Poetry Festival over a beer or two. Mark is Peterborough born and bred and a well-known ex-teacher, poet, rapper and battle rapper. His work is both funny, poignant and very popular online with much viral content. Mark's alter ego is the Count of Monty Gristo, a name he uses during battle raps. As an ex-teacher, Mark writes poetry aimed at a youth audience including the following lines from this poem, some of which could apply to parkrun:

What is special?

> teachers, leaders
> nurses, writers
> tight rope walkers
> taxi drivers
> scientists and
> astronauts
> and those who play
> and practice sports
> and those who speak up
> standing tall
> and those who listen
> that's not all

Intrigued by the Count of Monty Gristo's battle rapping, I composed this short haiku-like poem:

> battle rap
>
> the rhythm
>
> of a run
>
> no comeback
>
> from the heron

Bela Legosi's dead happy

14. THE CINDER TRACK, WHITBY

Run Report: For the dead travel fast, 01/01/2022

"I am Dracula; and I bid you welcome, Mr. Harker, to my house." Bram Stoker (1897)

The rundead need stimulation. I've grown fat over the centuries lounging around my Transylvanian castle and prowling the streets of Whitby after that incident with the ship and the hound. The new parkrun in town has perked me up. Think of all those parkrun tourists staying in local guest houses, a veritable banquet of blood. But no! I shall have the last laugh. The centuries will allow me to beat any record that the uber-tourists set! I won't convert any parkrunners to my vampire army for the dead don't run. Domination of the parkrun universe will be mine, forever.

I decide to risk the Cinder Track on New Year's Day with sunglasses, hat and sun cream for protection from the daylight. Leaving my coffin before sunrise, I fly bat-style to Whitby Sixth Form to meet the three sisters. They're helping to marshal this morning, in onesies to protect them from the UV, along with 17 volunteers. Rundead director this morning is Matt Hewison. I scour the assembled crowd of gothic ghouls for Ran Helsing. He must be at the start-line, probably still bench presses 120 these days. Those darn tourists the Harkers may be here too. They're fans of the 1932 film. Thankfully, Bela Lugosi's dead. I much preferred Christopher Lee's Hammer interpretation anyway.

The Cinder Track run begins at nine, sharp as a fang. Luckily for me, most of the route is tree-lined shade but I take care on the open Larpool Viaduct just after the start which has spectacular views of Whitby including my beloved abbey on the hill. I remember when it was just a windswept hilltop, ideal for a count wishing to spend eternity in peace. Thanks to Bram Stoker I'm a star attraction in the town. Now I get the annual goth invasion at Halloween. Simply dreadful! That god-awful parkrun poet Tim Gardiner is running here today, just ahead of me with a tacky cape and Nosferatu t-shirt. He's one I won't be converting to the ranks of the rundead, he'd bore me to tears with his existential street poetry and tales of Bauhaus mosh pits.

The run to halfway is on the gently sloping railway line closed in 1965, acquiring around 150 ft. of elevation along Stainsacre Lane to the turnaround which is a silent killer to the legs and lungs. Then it's all downhill, get your breath back and lengthen that stride. The course is nothing compared to my old 5K in the Carpathians, 1000 ft. of elevation up the precipice to the castle. No hounds of hell (barkrunners) were taking part as the parkrun does not allow dogs but a werewolf was howling in Cock Mill Wood along Stainsacre Beck. I did think about the morphing into a dog trick again but it's lost originality in the years since Stoker's novel blew my cover. There is a slight uphill part of the track to the finish by the oak tree where we started. That tree has too much potential for stake making in my opinion. The first finishers were James Anderson (17:45) and Kani Hinshelwood (21:27) out of a field of 171 runners and walkers which is a new record for the event and matches the road which runs past Whitby Sixth Form (A171). There were 112 first timers, tourists bolstering the ranks and thankfully 101 runners beat the poet (29:23). The marshals were horrendously positive, the stench of garlic was almost overbearing out there and most crossed themselves as I passed by! I thought they could see right through me....

And then, the worst possible outcome. Checking my cape, the barcode is missing. The paper scrap must have blown away in the Whitby wind. Why did no-one tell me about the phone app!

Sadly, this morning the Dracula name, like my reflection in a mirror, is missing. Face fixed with a furious gaze, I decide to fly back to the abbey and get some sleep. This parkrun will pay a heavy price on my return in a couple of centuries…

The Count's Tourist Tip-off –
Whitby Abbey and Bobbit's Hole

Here's my top place to visit if you're making a weekend of it. If you must visit Whitby Abbey then run up the 199 steps, my personal best is 47 seconds. I'd rather you followed the Cinder Trail to Robin Hood's Bay to recreate the famous trek of Mina Murray and Lucy Westenra. When on the beach at Robin Hood's Bay, it's well worth having a look in Bobbit's Hole Cave and keeping an eye out for the seals.

Poetry Corner

Caedmon College in Whitby is named after the first known English poet, Caedmon (c. 657 – 684). Caedmon was a Northumbrian who looked after animals at Streonæshalch which is now Whitby Abbey. Only nine lines of his poetry exist, despite his original ignorance of "the art of song." His only remaining lines come from a dream in which he composed them empowered by god, according to the 8th-century historian Bede. Caedmon's poetry is like holy water to me so I won't repeat it. Instead, I overheard that punctilious parkrun poet spouting haiku-like lines near the oak:

> who sees scars
> concealed
> by a cowl

viaduct views
on tiptoe

distant
abbey arches
beneath our feet

steam rises
but not from engines

if the dead
travel fast
over cinder

the living pass
no slower

Frosty morning at Monsal Trail

15. MONSAL TRAIL

Run Report: A bridge too far, 15/01/2022

The Peak District is undoubtedly one of my favourite places in England. In the White Peak, so called because of its limestone geology, Monsal Head affords breath-taking views along Monsal Dale and the Wye Valley. The 91 metre long Headstone Viaduct on the former Midland Railway crosses the river and is part of the Monsal Trail, a popular route with walkers, runners and cyclists. When the railway was built in the 1870s, the famous art critic John Ruskin campaigned against the environmental damage it would cause so that "every fool in Buxton can be in Bakewell in half an hour."

Monsal Trail parkrun was formerly Bakewell parkrun which utilised a different course heading north-west from Hassop Station towards Monsal Head. Monsal Trail parkrun follows the southern extent of the old railway on a flat(ish) section from Hassop Station and is a fast out and back course with some spectacular views of the hills and several bridges to run under. Starting at the picnic area, you first pass the wonderfully named Pineapple House Farm and under the first bridge. It's then a fast downhill section to Bakewell Station which is quite an eerily stark, but not unappealing brick building with dark doors and prominent chimneys. The route descends gradually down Castle Hill to the turnaround point before the gentle climb back to the finish at the picnic area. My previous parkrun was at the old railway line of the Cinder Track in Whitby which had an uphill outward half then back downhill to the finish. Monsal Trail is Whitby in reverse! Whatever the elevation profile, old railway line parkruns are among my favourites.

On arrival, the temperature was a bracing minus five, one of the hardest frosts I've run in. It felt like stepping out of the wardrobe into Narnia! Run director Andy Mellor informed us at the briefing that there were five frozen puddles we must avoid. The parkrun had been cancelled the week before due to icy conditions so we were grateful to be running at all. I wish I'd listened to the advice of fell runner Mike Nolan (2nd finisher, 18:31) before the start to take it easy on the downhill first half, otherwise the gradual incline of the second half will be a struggle. The running marshal (not an Arnie film!) keeping everyone to the left was a nice touch as the ghost train of parkrunners did tend to wander. Once finished, the parkrun special (drink and Bakewell tart) in the café was good value and I was made to feel most welcome by volunteers, Margaret and Richard McCall.

Event 117 had 182 finishers and was made possible by 18 fantastic volunteers. The first finishers defying the frost to record superb times were Charlie Baker (17:41) and Claire Elizabeth Biercamp (20:09). Yvonne Twelvetree (VW70-74) ran 25:57 for a stellar age grade of 87.22%. Congratulations to the 25 athletes who recorded new course PBs, an excellent achievement given the Siberian weather. There were no milestones but 15 athletes completed their first parkrun and began what is hopefully a lifelong journey. Personally speaking, 128 runners beat the pontificating poet (29:57). I paid for the early pace of the first half as foretold in Mike's pre-parkrun prophecy!

Tim's Tourist Tip-off – Curbar Edge and Thorpe Cloud

Here's my top places to visit if you're making a weekend of it. Around 15 minutes from Hassop Station is Curbar Edge near Baslow. A drive up to the gritstone escarpments of Curbar Edge and adjacent Baslow Edge is well worth it for the views across the Derwent Valley. The high gothic stones drop steeply away from heather moorland into woodland. Why not climb the Eagle Stone if you're agile enough. It was said men from Baslow had to climb the rock to prove their suitability for marriage! I also had a quick clamber up Thorpe Cloud (summit 287 m) at Dovedale after the parkrun where I was above the dense fog with stunning views from the rocky outcrop. A rare double sunset can be seen over Thorpe Cloud around the summer solstice, when the sun sets over the hill summit and then briefly reappears from its steep northern slope and sets again!

Poetry Corner

As an ode to Monsal Trail, here's a light-hearted poem:

Mind the Gap

>the 09:00 service
>from Hassop to Bakewell
>leaves from Platform 1
>parkrunners are advised
>that there is no buffet car

>athletes are reminded
>that luggage left at the start
>will be attended by volunteers
>please do not leave luggage unattended
>as it may be removed and sold

>this is a security message
>if you see something

that doesn't look right
don't panic, no one
looks good when running

special announcement
the runner approaching
does not stop here
please keep well back
from the right edge of the path

this parkrun operates
a no barcode no time policy
checks are in operation
please have your barcode
ready for inspection

and finally
mind the gap between
expectation and reality
seconds matters less
than effort

16. STOREYS FIELD

Run Report: The ridge of sighs, 29/01/2022

A spectacular sunrise greeted me as I left home in Manningtree on the Essex coast. The red and orange hues just before the sun poked over the horizon were so vivid that taking a photo would have ruined the moment. The early start was needed for a spot of parkrun tourism to Storey's Field, a trip of around 70 miles. I was looking forward to the parkrun, although the flare up of an old knee injury tempered the usual enthusiasm. My target of the Cowell Club (100 different parkrun events/locations) seems a long way off but I hope to be there by year end, injury permitting. I'm taking it one run at a time with very light training.

On arrival at Storey's Field, the most obvious concern for runners and walkers was the stiff breeze on an open course. The backdrop to the whole shebang were the brand-spanking new University of Cambridge buildings. The innovative Storey's Field Centre is contained within the new sustainable town of Eddington. The futuristic setting is how I imagine the first moon base to look, straight out of Kubrick's film 2001: A Space Odyssey. There are some monolithic art installations around so maybe this is where humanity evolves as foreseen by Arthur C. Clarke! The pleasant park hosts the three-lap course which sees runners and walkers utilising a firm gravel or tarmac surface underfoot. Storey's Field is an excellent parkrun for those feeling the need for speed or others wanting a route with no obvious hills or inclines. The actual route is hard to describe, although some say that it's a squashed figure of eight lap with a short section on the Ridgeway. For me it seems like one of those wire-loop games where you try and pass the hoop over the twisting metal without setting the buzzer off. A special mention should be made of one of the best sprint finishes (on the Ridgeway) I've come across with a downhill dash allowing a swift end to the suffering.

Event 25 saw a new attendance record of 384 finishers and was made possible by 25 fantastic volunteers. Storey's Field appears to be gaining in popularity quickly with a large catchment area, friendly volunteer team and the absence of hills! I'm sure it won't be long before the attendance record is smashed. There were 75 first timers, 45 different running clubs and 56 new personal bests. The first finishers defying the breeze to record superb times were Michael Baker (15:53) and Anna Klucnika (19:38). There were plenty of milestones: 10 Club (under 18) - Max Kullar and Alex Dixon; 25 Club – Adam Pattenden, Alan Slade and Elena Webb. Personally speaking, 279 runners beat the pained poet (30:33). I struggled with the fresh breeze like many others, the knees just about holding up but sore as hell for the rest of the day. Since restart whenever I've gone to a fast parkrun expecting a 'quick' time, I've tended to run slower than on a hilly one! C'est bizarre!

Tim's Tourist Tip-off – King's College and the Mathematical Bridge

After a lively chat with a volunteer about Cambridge University producing scientists while Oxford merely churns out politicians, I decided to take a trip from the nearby park and ride into the city centre. I made a beeline for the gothic architecture of King's College. It was one of my dad's favourite places and he'd always listen to Carols From King's every Christmas Eve. I guess some of his enthusiasm passed down a generation. After enough time had passed keeping off the grass and crocuses, the interwoven wood of the Mathematical Bridge of Queen's College was viewed from Silver Street. The bridge was first erected in 1749 and rebuilt in 1905. It's an example of a Voussoir Arch Bridge with all wooden elements held in place by compression from the force of gravity, a complicated engineering design hence its name. I didn't have time for a punt down the River Cam but those doing so will pass under the Bridge of Sighs which was built in 1831 and named after the famous Venice canal crosser which connects the Doge's Palace with a prison. I once had a conversation about the Bridge of Sighs with a friend, only to find out that they were talking about the Cambridge version, not Venice which I was referring to! Fascinating.

Poetry Corner

Having forgotten where the park and ride pick-up stop was, I decided to limp back to the car. I'm glad I did, passing snowdrops and primroses, early signs of the coming spring. Mistletoe was also in abundance on two trees on the Churchill College campus. Several running naturalists (not naturists!) including uber-tourist John Buchanan believe the parasitic plant to be more commonly seen these days. Inspired by all of this, I finish with a short, haiku-like poem:

more twists

and turns

than a labyrinth

my mind wanders

like mistletoe

17. SOHAM VILLAGE COLLEGE

Run Report: The Tannhäuser Gait, 12/02/2022

I've seen things you parkrunners wouldn't believe. But I've not seen a paper barcode on fire off the shoulder of Orion or a high-vis jacket glitter in the dark near the Tannhäuser Gate. There's just no off-world parkruns, no funding to set them up and the app doesn't work in deep space. The volunteer roster would be a weekly nightmare. Who's going to travel between systems every Saturday? But I'm not here just for parkrun, my knees only have a four-year life. My creator may be able to repair them. While waiting, Soham Village College seems like an appropriate place to run as it has a film studies course on which students analyse Blade Runner. They appreciate the dramatic pause here. However, I need to dodge the attentions of parkrun poet, Tim Gardiner, who'll be limping along near the back. I read his book, Glade Runner, while parked up in the Orion Nebula. It documents his tour of 50 UK parkruns before COVID-19 hit. He travelled less than 30000 km for that! Pah! What a puny effort, equivalent to only three quarters of the way around the earth's equator. The Glade Runner has been sent to retire me before my parkrun journey starts. Good luck with that mortal!

I managed to mingle with 52 assembled athletes and 21 fantastic volunteers before the start, although my naked torso did raise some eyebrows given the typical fenland wind chill. It's also hard to stuff a dove down these tight shorts! I was expecting rain but there's a strong breeze instead ruling out a post-parkrun monologue. The course is all on grass and is a three and a bit laps route that reminds me a little of the constellation Leo. The first half of each lap is run on grass around parkland dotted with old oaks. It is pretty muddy in places and contains the first summit in the Soham Alps (S1 is around 6 ft.). While nothing like the precipitous Catterhorn at Catton, I nearly stacked it on the first ascent. Eventually, we wind into the College buildings section which is labyrinthine in its twists and turns. Parts of it also remind me of the Star Wars trench run on the Death Star. There's also the second summit in the Soham Alps range (S2 around 4 ft.) to contend with.

After the first lap, I'm reminded of the words of my creator: the flame that burns twice as bright burns half as long. Which I think means don't go out too quick otherwise you'll blow up in the last mile! Never been my problem. Fiery the angels fell. Deep thunder rolled around their shoulders...burning with the fires of Orc. This is not one of the easier parkruns, the average run time of 32 mins reflecting the often windy and wet underfoot parkland sections.

There's no chance of the parkrun poet escaping me. Six! Seven! Go to hell or go to heaven. I'm aiming to finish first! We're not computers, we're physical! I see the parkrun poet in my sights, struggling yet again with those legs. He stumbles and falls on a muddy patch as I approach, silently. I could finish his parkrun journey here and now. No more tedious run reports. No more puns. No more spurious words that have little or nothing to do with parkrun. But I stretch a hand out and help the old boy up. This is no time to die. To mark the occasion, I release the dove from my shorts and watch the parkrun poet trot off. As there's no rain for profound soliloquies, I decide to continue to the finish.

The first finishers defying the breeze and mud were Ewan Taylor (19:07) and Claire Flack (28:45). Amusingly, 31 runners beat the pained parkrun poet (30:42). I had tea with uber- tourists from Yorkshire, John and Joanna Cassells who have both run 336 different UK parkruns to place 10th and 11th in the UK Most

Events Table, respectively. They truly have seen things you people wouldn't believe. I must also mention the sterling run of George Ginn (age cat 85-89).

Roy's Tourist Tip-off – St. Andrew's Church

Soham is where Olaudah Equiano, also known as Gustavus Vassa, married a local girl, Susannah Cullen, in St. Andrew's Church (first built 1180) in 1792. He was the first black British author and slavery abolitionist. Olaudah had been enslaved in Africa and transported to the Caribbean and sold to a Royal Navy Officer. His autobiography, The Interesting Narrative of the Life of Olaudah Equiano (1789), was a powerful document on the horrors of slavery. Olaudah's book was pivotal in attaining passage for the Slave Trade Act (1807) which abolished slavery.

Poetry Corner

Before I leave the system and return to Orion's Belt, I finish with a short, haiku-like poem:

>the black hole
>between strides
>pain free
>an oak branch
>still leafless

18. ROYAL TUNBRIDGE WELLS

Run Report: Exhausted of Tunbridge Wells, 19/02/2022

Dear parkrunners

Despite Storm Eunice wreaking havoc with my hanging baskets, I decided a pleasant trot around Dunorlan Park might take the mind off the necessary replacement cost. That the parkrun was on at all was due to the sterling efforts of volunteers in clearing up fallen branches along the undulatory course route and the event team's can-do attitude. The morning was a sunny Wealden one, the literal calm before the start. They say the strongest gust in England was 122 mph at The Needles on the Isle of Wight. Unfortunately, the wind returned during the parkrun, could it have been the so-called Sting Jet tail-end of the storm? The off-road part of the course was saturated in many places, making my choice of road shoes a rather poor one. I mean, what was I thinking? The upper part of the route resembled a cross between the Grimpen Mire and the Dead Marshes. The trick was to navigate boggy patches more cannily on the second lap. Apparently, during the summer the course dries out significantly and is much faster. I love the High Weald with its Oast Houses and wooded hillsides so need little excuse to return.

Undulating was a rather interesting choice of wording in the course info. That finish on Heartbreak Hill resembled the Lhotse Face. Admittedly, it's no Catterhorn (Norfolk) but after the exertions of two laps, it's a killing blow. Of the different global courses I've run, including the hellish Great Yarmouth North Beach slog-fest and several hilly ones, Tunbridge Wells was by the far the hardest yet, reflected in my third slowest parkrun time and slowest 5K in four years. The triad of despair (wind, soft ground and hills) was the perfect storm for the 188 athletes although incredibly 11 parkrunners recorded course pbs. Well done to them all! First finishers James Sarre (20:11) and Lisa Knight (23:30) defied the swamp to record superb times in the conditions. Poetry wise, 136 parkrunners beat the poet (34:17) who should stick to writing!

The marshals today were wonderfully positive as always including the comedian who said it was all downhill at the end of the lap and Laurence Bunnett who talked about the history of Dunorlan Park. We were well-stocked with 41 volunteers (Hugh Stephenson reached a commendable 50 volunteering credits) with a hive of activity at the start led by run director Robin Barwick. The view from the start funnel around 60 ft. above the lake is breath-taking showing the extent of the fine parkland landscape designed by Robert Marnock for Henry Reed in the 1800s with 'harmony in nature' in mind. Reed's elegant Dunorlan House was used during World War II by soldiers who allegedly shot at the statues during target practice. Sadly, Reed's mansion was demolished in 1958 with only the stone terrace near the parkrun start remaining.

It was a rare privilege to run 'with' my son again in his brand-spanking new 50 top. That he was within sight at the end of the first lap meant he had either listened to my lecture on pacing a parkrun, or he'd stayed up too late on the Xbox. It was tricky to stay on your feet today and a chap behind my son went for a Burton on the second lap and crossed the line covered in gloop. The park's geese and ducks were more suited to the course this morning.

Tim's Tourist Tip-off – Wellington Rocks

With legs covered in mud we ventured into the former spa town. The obligatory Pantiles walk was followed by a trip up to

Wellington Rocks which are sandstone boulders overlooking Tunbridge Wells. The rocks form part of the sandstone ridge of the High Weald that runs across southern England from Hampshire to Kent. The geology and hilly nature of the Tunbridge Wells area is what makes the parkrun a tough one but also creates the varied landscape of high importance for wildlife. On the way home, we took the road to West Malling and played a game of spot the Oast House. These hop-drying buildings with distinctive conical roofs are a characteristic feature of the High Weald and Kent generally. Oast Houses are now redundant due to industrial drying of hops and many have been converted into residential houses.

Poetry Corner

Far from being disgusted of Tunbridge Wells, I finish with a short, haiku-like poem for Dunorlan Park and the High Weald:

> runner's dilemma
> the mire or cut
> the corner

> shame the shoes
> don't dry like hops

19. CHALKWELL BEACH

Run Report: Seagrass and spaniels in the city, 26/02/2022

It was a perfectly sunny morning for Chalkwell Beach parkrun's second birthday with a gentle onshore breeze. The stunning panorama of the Thames Estuary is the first thing you notice on the prom. The pier stretches out into the expanse of the Thames to the east and you can just make out Hadleigh Castle to the west. The north Kent coast is a far-off world of hills and industry. If you're lucky, the haunting call of the curlew can be heard from the mudflats at low tide. With the clear improvements to seafront infrastructure and parkland in recent years, the parkrun is another feather in the cap of Southend City. On Tuesday 1st March, City status will be officially recognised with a royal visit.

To kick off the birthday celebrations, Kieran gave an enthusiastic run briefing throwing some serious shapes before the exercise-inspired fun began. This morning we had pacers. The one I was determined to keep up with was 28 minute Claire Kirkland. As usual, I went out far too quick for my current fitness and Claire started to pull away around the mile mark. The course takes you to Adventure Island and back and is fast and flat. I was spurred on by Wally James's music in the first mile creating a chilled atmosphere for the sunny, almost-spring morning in Southend. A spaniel with a topknot was perhaps the most unexpected sight on the prom!

Chalkwell Beach legend Dave Petrie was at his post and received a rapturous fanfare from the peloton. On the homeward leg the pack had noticeably thinned out around me and the 29 and 30 minute pacers came and went as the old faderoo set in again as the knees protested. I did manage to sprint and keep the 31 min guy at bay though! I made many new friends today notably tourist David Lock of Fordy Runs who recorded his first sub-25 parkrun, congratulations to him. Over a post-run drink we discussed all of the parkruns we'd run and were planning to visit. My new favourite parkrunner is Neil Claxton who battled his way around the course and got the biggest cheer I've heard for a runner entering the finish funnel. A local legend just like Wilko Johnson.

Post-parkrun I decided to hobble down to Southend Pier. I've lived in Essex for the best part of 25 years and have never been to the end of the 1.33 miles long structure which is the longest pleasure pier in the world. As I trod the boards, the tide beneath was ebbing and the mudflats were scattered with curlews, gulls and oystercatchers. The perfect accompaniment to a tourist trip to Southend. Pint downed in the pier end bar, I had one last goal: find some seagrass on the beach near the parkrun start. Seagrasses form the meadows of the sea, the only flowering plants in the world's oceans. Seagrass meadows are important for protecting flood defences (reducing wave erosion), providing habitat for seahorses and fish (amongst other marine species) and for removing carbon from the atmosphere. I knew there were extensive meadows of seagrass at Old Leigh but had never found it as far east as Chalkwell Beach. Several large patches of eelgrass (a type of seagrass) were found around 200 m west of the start/finish area laying prostrate on the sand awaiting the incoming tide to be set afloat like green ribbons. Chalkwell Beach parkrun is not alone in having seagrass in close proximity, the hilly Ganavan Sands (visited last August) on the west coast of Scotland has some too. At Chalkwell Beach eelgrass is mentioned on the foreshore information board opposite the Crowstone Monument and forms part of the largest seagrass meadow in south-east England. Chalkwell Beach is a parkrun with an ecological heart.

20. STRATFORD-UPON-AVON

Run Report: The taming of the shoe, 12/03/2022

A parkrun play with Rosencrantz and Guildenstern (Hamlet) and Shakespeare quotes.

Act 1, Scene 1. A park somewhere in Stratford

Parkrunners assemble at the Recreation Ground, Stratford-upon-Avon. The River Avon flows gently along the edge of the course ruffled by the witches' wind. Rowers are cajoled by a vocal cox disturbing geese and swans in the reeds. Spring is well underway with white blackthorn blossoms arching over the paths, falling like confetti in the stiff breeze. In Stratford 'tis a perfect morning for parkrun on a flat, hard surface. Be quiet the lickspittle who has yet to rise.

Rosencrantz: I'm glad we made good our escape from the executioner!

Guildenstern: Yes, bid me run, and I will strive with things impossible. Something is rotten in the state of Denmark. So much so we cannot parkrun there.

Run director Paul Hodges gives a rousing speech. He dost read the rules and atmos. The 31 volunteers exit stage left to take up their positions. Runners and walkers take flight at nine.

Rosencrantz: It be a three-lap affair of the park in a clockwise fashion.

Guildenstern: The Royal Shakespeare Theatre can be seen on the left as we traverse the Avon path. It's looking a bit black over Bill's mother's Rosencrantz….

Act 1, Scene 2. Lapping it up

The duo wind their merry way around the first lap. Despite Guildenstern's portentous utterance, the storm stayeth away.

Guildenstern: Brevity is the soul of parkrun.

Rosencrantz: Though this be madness, yet there is method in't. Faith, I ran when I saw others run.

Guildenstern: Listen to many, speak to few. Make those few the marshals. Bring a little cheer to their morn.

Rosencrantz: One may smile, and smile, and be a marshal. They are spared a run in these late-Tudor robes.

Act 2, Scene 1. The poet's ghost

Guildenstern: I do believe the executioner has caught up with us Rosencrantz.

Rosencrantz: To flee, or not to flee, that is the question. Run, master, run!

Guildenstern: Alas, poor poet, I knew him and Horatio: a fellow of infinite jest and little running talent.

Rosencrantz: Ah, his offence is rank, it smells to heaven. It may be just his road shoes. What hell befalls those who mistook the parkrun poet's ghost for the executioner?

Guildenstern: Our wills and fates do so contrary run. The parkrun poet must suffer for his art.

Rosencrantz: The rest is silence. That stewed prune is like the ghost in Hamlet.

Act 2, Scene 2. Perchance to pong

After a circuitous three laps easily evading the parkrun poet's ghost, Rosencrantz and Guildenstern enter the funnel and collect their finish tokens. They are reminded not to take them home.

Rosencrantz: The lady doth protest too much, methinks.

Guildenstern: But relinquish these curious barcodes we must. And then to nap, perchance to dream of sub-30.

The daring duo decide to play a quick game of ping pong and wait for the results notification. While they chase the ball on the wind, a fallen runner is helped to the finish funnel by marshals and run director Paul Hodges, an act which embodies the spirit of parkrun. This morning, 277 athletes ran or walked the parkrun. First finishers were Jessica Sheppard (20:17) and Will Senior (17:07) with sprightly times.

Rosencrantz (yawning): I could compose a sonnet. How about one for the lovers on the Ferris wheel?

Guildenstern: What is a Ferris wheel? Who is Ferris? Besides, I think our doggerel is second only to that of the parkrun poet. Ruin not, what has been a joyous morn.

The parkrun poet's ghost (materialising): How darest thou insult my musings unable worms! Besides, there is much to say about this parkrun. Dean Murray and David Howard completed their 100th runs, while John Raby and Tony Stott joined the 50 Club. Five runners earned their 25 t-shirt: Roland Hancock, Margaret Harries, William Mann, Nikki Pearson and Max Robbins. And lastly, young Alfie Musk celebrated joining the Junior 10 Club with a swift 22:02.

Rosencrantz: It's the last night of Much Ado this evening in the Royal Shakespeare Theatre. Shall I book thou tickets?

Guildenstern: Oh, Rosencrantz. You knowest I love Bill's tragicomedies with the knockaround material.

Their iPhones beep in synchrony. The results' email has arrived.

Rosencrantz: May fire reign down on my aching glutes! Another sub-30 gone begging. How can I run better?

Guildenstern: Wisely, and slow. They stumble that run fast.

The parkrun poet's ghost (dematerialising): Ha! Out of my sight knaves, thou dost infect my eyes!

Tim's Tourist Tip-off

This being the birthplace of England's most famous poet, William Shakespeare (1564-1616), there really is only one place to visit. Check out Shakespeare's Birthplace in Henley Street, a 16th century, half-timbered house with a beautiful cottage garden which will be full of butterflies and bees in summer on the wide assortment of flowering herbs. The Bard was born here in 1564. Then visit the Church of the Holy Trinity to see his grave. The third and final stop is Anne Hathaway's (wife) house which is a little out of town.

Poetry Corner

I bid you farewell with this short haiku-like poem inspired by Stratford-upon-Avon, in the 405th spring since Shakespeare's death:

come again, spring

>after the run
>I buy a cheap bookmark
>for my Juliet
>in the gift shop
>shelter from rain outside
>Shakespeare's birthplace
>still homeless
>people
>forget flowers
>in the daffodil garden

21. WINCHESTER

Run Report: The wayfarer's stroll, 26/03/2022

The return of Sir Runalot

He was there at the first Winchester parkrun on 27th April 2013 despite the time machine crash on nearby Winnall Moors Nature Reserve, scattering water voles into River Itchen watercress. North Walls Park is located on the edge of the South Downs National Park, a finger of which pokes into the city along the Itchen Valley. Today, Sir Runalot got the dashboard co-ordinates right and landed on the part of the course they call the Island which is surrounded by attractive waterways streaked with the green ribbons of aquatic plants. The morning was warm and sunny. Brimstone and peacock butterflies were on the wing early. A gentle breeze provided the perfect morning for running. Runalot had every chance of beating his personal best, the holy grail for parkunners. Granted, the armour doesn't help, clanking along is less than ideal. But his chivalric code, gained around King Arthur's Round Table which now adorns Winchester Great Hall in the city centre, prevented him from anything other than full honorific attire.

Runalot is a fan of the course's twists and turns and flat nature. It's a two-lapper comprising circuits of the cricket and rugby pitches and a bridge crossing onto the Island where walkers and runners have one foot in the South Downs National Park if they hug the Itchen path. On the Island runners and walkers are surrounded on all sides by water with the green-streaked Itchen and chalky ditches feeding off it. The parkrun course is almost Venetian as it passes the Bowls Club and turns back towards the start and finish areas, canal-like dykes darting off here and there with arching bridges. It's a watery, tree-lined course that Runalot enjoys greatly, hence the return. Others had travelled from as far away as South Africa to participate in the throng of 331 athletes, looked after by 34 volunteers good and true. The aptly named Joe Winchester tail-walked with Lynn McKeague. Michael Hollis kindly had time to talk chalk rivers with Runalot before the off.

The run itself was a rather tough affair. On a balmy morning a suit of armour was the worst kind of masochistic fancy dress, the profusely sweaty knight grateful for the shade of tall riverside trees. He didn't need to worry about the quicker runners, first finishers Naomi Findlay (21:15) and Joe Driscoll (17:30) left the parkrun peloton behind. At the rear, a puppy was enticed along the finish strait with a bag of dog treats!

To Runalot's amusement, his beloved honours system doesn't mean anything at parkrun. All parkrunners are created equal. Except for the following who are now entitled to cool milestone t-shirts - 50 Club: Stefan Kemp and Andrew Rice, 25 Club: Peter Dowson, Leon Hutchings, Adrian Letty, Aleasha Mallon, Grant McKnight and Alex Walmsley.

Runalot's Tourist Tip-off

After the volunteers dispersed, Runalot trotted off for a walk leaving the time machine parked on the Island. Following the course of the river through Winnall Moors nature reserve is the best way to wind into the city. Reedbeds and wet woodland merge seamlessly with each other. After some odd looks in Subway, Runalot enjoyed fish spotting at Winchester City Mill (National Trust) before dragging his plate metal bling up to Winchester Great Hall. King Arthur's Round Table presented to the public like the world's largest dartboard raised an eyebrow and reminded him that he must be back in Camelot by nightfall. Back at Winchester City Mill, he took the riverside path to the

Hospital of St. Cross through lush water meadows. They'd offer the Wayfarer's Dole (bread and beer) to an old friend, surely? Arriving, Runalot was greeted with blank faces. Apparently, long dead knights are not hot property in the social media age. In no mood for the Spanish Inquisition, Runalot accepted the Wayfarer's Dole for it was an unseasonably warm day and he needed sustenance.

Lumbering over to St. Catherine's Hill, he found cowslips and primroses in abundance. The historic Miz Maze cut into chalk turf baffled Runalot as it had for centuries although he resisted the temptation to cheat his way to the middle. Winchester City and Itchen water meadows provided the vista for the long walk back to the time machine. Much had changed since King Arthur's time. The bustle of modern living was not for world-weary knights such as Runalot. A parking ticket attached to the time machine's hatch only highlighted the grievance.

Poetry Corner

Runalot scrawled a short haiku-like poem on the back of the parking ticket and pinned it to a tree:

lying
by the watercress beds
a bee mimic

runners give motion
to the morning

Anyone for darts? The Winchester round table

22. CASTLE PARK

Run Report: The Lizard Pepys, 02/04/2022

"and so to Bishop's Stafford [sic]. The ways mighty full of water so as hardly to be passed."

Samuel Pepys. Diarist. 23 May 1668.

You're crenelated, parkrunner!

My way to Castle Park in Bishop's Stortford was less full of water than in the sub-aquatic times of the 17th century diarist Samuel Pepys. Castle Park is full of history though. A motte (mound) has the ruins of Waytemore Castle on the summit. This parkrun reminded me of Clare Castle in Suffolk where a sprint up to the summit of the motte is a must-do post-parkrun to bag another nihilistic Strava segment! It's possible the castle started as a Celtic barrow (grave mound) before the motte and bailey began in the time of William the Conqueror. King John made improvements in the 13th century, crenelation (also known as castellation or building typical castle battlements) was undertaken in the 14th century before the castle was damaged after the Civil War. Its final use was as a prison in the 17th century. Be respectful as you're probably running over human remains! A large number of bones were discovered in the 1990s suggesting that a medieval hospital may have been present on the site.

My way to Bishop's Stortford was full of frost rather than the water noted by Pepys. A crowd of 199 athletes gathered to run the two-lap circuit of Castle Park. I was over the moon to meet Noel Thatcher (and Yumi, his wife), a Paralympian athlete of 6 games (5 gold medals). Noel is also a Japanophile (lover of all things Japanese) so we talked of cherry blossom (sakura in Japanese) and haiku poetry before the off. From here things went downhill on a personal level with a flare up of an old calf injury meaning a modified jog/limp technique for the last 2 miles. I discovered that by swinging my right injured leg through in a straightened fashion like a pendulum, I could use the unaffected left leg to hop along and do the work. It was a shambling Long John Silver method to avoid putting too much weight on the affected leg which was quicker than merely trudging. A total shambles and another injury to add to the list but I got round in no small part thanks to the enthusiastic encouragement of the marshals (26 volunteers today) and other runners. Far ahead of me, the first finishers were Ruby Featherstone (21:29) and Sam Pedley (17:08). Robin Rickard joined the 50 Club and Mary Cattermole earned her 25 Club vest, congratulations to both of them.

Having suffered for the run, I was in need of a post-parkrun pickup. The tea and coffee van provided that nicely as did a sluggish trawl around the castle ruins and motte. The drooping yellow heads of cowslips were in full bloom, a lovely sign of spring. I also saw a common lizard dart into a hole in the earth. We shared a beautiful moment where the lizard poked its head out and watched me watching it. That's a zen haiku moment right there! The River Stort is a lovely boundary for the parkrun too, the goat willow blossoms arching over the flowing water.

Tim's Tourist Tip-off

The best advice is to stay in Castle Park for this one. Take time for the short ascent to the summit of the castle motte and enjoy the ruins and views of the parkland. A peaceful moment you won't regret. You might even see a lizard or two!

Poetry Corner

The Bishop's Stortford area is the residence of a friend of mine, Mary Epworth, who is an esteemed folk/prog rock singer and musician who I met because of our shared love of glow-worms which are notably found along the parkrun courses at Clare Castle, Rendlesham Forest and Sizewell in the east. Mary's poignant lyrics for the superb 2015 track, Long Gone, beautifully describe the state of my running:

> Long gone, most beloved
> The road has bowed away
> And I cannot rise above it

I finish with a couple of cherry blossom haiku (traditional spring poems) for all who love Japan:

> blossom
> for the path
> we travel
> spring breeze
> take it or leave it

23. CONWY

Run Report: Day of the Jackdaw, 09/04/2022

Through the words of a fictional resident of Great Britain's smallest house in Conwy.

Blast it! I've cracked my head on that low beam. Again. The estate agents said this house was small and they weren't joking. A lick of red paint attracts the tourists who poke their noses into my residence for a paltry quid. I've had to abandon my weekly run along the top of the high town walls due to an ongoing knee issue. I miss the shortcut across Mr. Dalton's roof. He'd always rush out and fill the air with expletives before his false teeth hit the deck! The absence of wall and roof running meant that I became accustomed to jogging circuits of my 1.8 m x 3.05 m ground floor, roughly 515 laps to complete the 5K!

Understandably, it was something of a relief when a parkrun started in 2015. The route is an attractive out and back one starting at the RSPB car park with its sweeping panorama of the Conwy Estuary and Carneddau mountains which have the only population of wild horses in the UK. The riverside course allows a good glimpse of Conwy Castle with a hard surface underfoot for the speedsters. The only undulation is the bridge over the railway where the run narrows, constrained by the high sides of the structure. As you head towards Deganwy, the full force of any north-westerly wind is felt by runners and marshals at Windy Point, the only consolation here is that the run back to the finish funnel will be wind assisted. I enjoy it, it's certainly better than wearing the carpet out. This morning we had 200 athletes taking part looked after by 26 volunteers. There was even some English bore calling himself the parkrun poet, accompanied by his son Joseph. The poet is one to trip up with my giant feet. I'm 6 feet

3 inches tall after all. Large for a Jackdaw (person born within Conwy town walls).

In the briefing, run director Clive Nadin led a tribute to Gilbert Gillan, a regular Conwy parkrunner who sadly passed away after a short illness having run 89 parkruns and 59 virtual parkruns. Many of his club friends were here today. The record he leaves is a fine one with a superb pb of 22:47 (age cat VM65-69). A runner to inspire of us all.

Gill Thompson ran her 200th parkrun with a consistent record (pb 27:00, best age grade 75.6%) of sub-30 times. Jose Eduardo Vega Perez and Richard Morgan both ran their 100th parkruns and are eligible for the coveted black milestone vest. Shon Jones ran his 50th parkrun and earned the striking scarlet vest for the milestone. Michael Hayton and Megan Hughes ran their 25th parkruns, Megan celebrating with a new pb of 27:22. The first finishers were Amy McKechnie (20:32) and Tom Carter (17:51). Congratulations to all runners!

The parkrun is best rounded off with a visit to the RSPB's café with fine views. From the café windows, the yellow nodding heads of cowslips suggested spring, while the view of the snow-capped Carneddau mountains hinted that the winter had yet to release its grip on North Wales. In the corner, the parkrun poet was scribbling some pretentious drivel. Apparently, as of today he's written run reports for 50 different parkruns.

Tim's Tourist Tip-off

Look around my tiny house on the quay if you want, it's apparently the smallest in Great Britain. There's plenty of far larger places to visit including Conwy Castle (built in the 13th century by Edward I of England), Aberconwy Abbey, Aberconwy House (14th century merchant's house) and of course you must take a walk around the town walls, peeping into people's gardens and windows from above if that's your kind of thing! Further afield why not visit Anglesey and the village with the long name (58 letters): Llanfairpwllgwyngyllgogerychwyrndrobwllllantysiliogogogoch. For the more adventurous Snowdon is worth the trek to the summit (1085 m) although leave a couple of days between summiting and the parkrun to allow SnowDOMS to pass. Or better still, do it after! And don't expect a view from the summit!

Poetry Corner

Nearby Colwyn Bay was the birthplace of Timothy Dalton who played James Bond in The Living Daylights (1987) and Licence to Kill (1989). Apparently, he looked around my house when I was out once and remarked that it was a Walther PPK sized property (i.e. small). Terry Jones of Monty Python fame was also born in the area. Britain's tiniest house lends itself to the world's smallest poems so I finish with a couple of Japanese-style haiku to celebrate the area's famous sons:

satire

the life

of clouds

not every sky

is grey

The stunning Conwy parkrun

24. NORTH WALSHAM

Run Report: The Second Battle of North Walsham, 16/04/2022

Told by the ghost of Geoffrey Litster
(leader of Norfolk rebels in Peasants' Revolt, 1381)

The Battle of North Walsham in June 1381 was a defeat for my rebellious peasants taking on the forces of Henry le Despenser, Bishop of Norwich, in the last major skirmish of the Peasants' Revolt. This morning 136 parkrunners gather for a decisive confrontation with the course meandering (over 60 turns!) along the attractive oak-lined perimeter of the school playing field and War Memorial Park. It's two and a half laps taking in the mild undulations of the grassy terrain and the North Walsham Needle with its precipitous peak near the eastern park entrance! On this spring morning, cherry blossoms (known as Sakura in Japan) add colour to the park. How many runners and walkers notice the totem-pole turn in the park before you shimmy down the narrow, hedged path? More on that later.

After run director Sonya Powley finishes the run briefing, I step up to deliver a rousing speech to the assembled rebels (25 running clubs) ready to commit body, mind and soul to combatting wet grass. Pleasantries dealt with; I quickly move on to chivvying up the runners and walkers for The Second Battle of North Walsham. There must be no surrender to the twists and turns of the labyrinthine route. Time has no meaning here only how you face the challenge. When your calf muscles burn and your lungs are fit to burst, will you push on to victory? For that is what makes a parkrunner for the ages. What we do this morning will echo through parkrun history.

After a rallying cry for the 28 volunteers, the horde is off around the course. In the early skirmishes, runners and walkers hold their own. Only on the second lap does the band fragment sparring with the lumpy ground and winding route. The fastest rebels this morning are Nathan McCann (18:30) and Melanie Tindale (24:07), risking it all out front. In the peloton, Travis Neenan (29:20) came through a tough clash with the course to finish strongly. Nordic walker Chris Trenholm (46:59) bravely fought off the tail-walkers to storm through to the finish funnel unscathed. Roughly half the field beat the poet who ran his fastest time (29:06) since March 2020 on his 75th different global parkrun. We were lucky parkrun veteran Paul Woodyatt chose North Walsham as his 500th parkrun, his journey starting in 2008. Massive congratulations to Paul who now has the honour of wearing the coveted blue running vest.

All rebels made it around cheered on by the spirited resistance of the marshals. An Easter Hat was even on display! The sight of a totem-pole style sculpture carved into the trunk of a 120-year-old oak tree was heartening. The rural figures on the tree standing on each other's shoulders represent a community struggle to reach a common goal. Not only is it apt for commemorating the peasants' struggle in 1381 but also for the community spirit needed to get events like North Walsham parkrun off the ground. Parkrun is the very embodiment of all that is good in society at a time when things are darkening again. We must hope that North Walsham parkrun continues to bring runners and walkers together for years to come. A list of today's radical rebels is found at the end of the run report, time freely given to the cause as always.

When all parkrun paraphernalia is packed up and the parkland returns to quiet recreational pursuits once more, I vanish back to the battlefield marked with a stone cross near the water towers. Who knows when I will return?

Tim's Tourist Tip-off

Why not stay and have a coffee in North Walsham itself? The attractive Market Cross is a listed building while the ruined church of St. Nicholas is also worth a stroll around. The Great Fire of North Walsham on 25 June 1600 destroyed 118 homes, 70 shops and the Market Cross. Luckily, the town was rebuilt to what you see now. One of North Norfolk's gems.

Poetry Corner

Following on from last week's Conwy parkrun, I finish with a couple of Japanese-style haiku to celebrate the parkrun:

> grass dew
> yet pollen dusts
> a bee's knees

> skirting the totem
> butterfly and sunspot

25. STREET

Run Report: parkrun pyramid stage, 30/04/2022

A festival of running and walking

It was a warm and sunny spring day, no festival washout or mud fest this year. Consequently, there was a good gathering of festival goers (80 athletes). I'd travelled from Manningtree in Essex for a weekend of Baltane (Gaelic May Day festival) celebrations in nearby Glastonbury and Street was the obvious choice for a parkrun tourist looking for some morning entertainment. The course is full of twists and turns and is all on grass. It's relatively flat with a couple of short inclines, the most notable being the precipitous Street Summit in the south-east corner! But after the ascent, open that stride and head in a Torwards direction. In winter they tell me that the course can get muddy but today it was dry with fairly short grass throughout. There's a very short, wooded section (enjoy the brief shade!) and spectacular views of the marshy Somerset Levels with hills puncturing the horizon in all directions.

The unique landscape of the Somerset Levels is best viewed from the top of Glastonbury Tor (more on that later) where a good view of the fields, hills and wetlands can be obtained. If you look eastwards from the tower, you can just make out the Pyramid Stage at Worthy Farm. A range of rare insect species are to be found in the marshland nature reserves of the Levels including the Large Marsh Grasshopper which is also seen on boggy ground near Moors Valley parkrun in Dorset.

Festival running order:

The First Finishers

First up on the parkrun pyramid stage, The First Finishers, a local band with the lightning quick Matthew Lusby (16:19, new PB) and Amelie Cook (21:28) who proved that running on grass doesn't have to be a slow affair. A rousing set full of superb running technique and no small amount of effort.

Emma Powell and the PBs

Like most ska bands, Emma Powell and the PBs had 13 members this morning (with lead singer Emma belting out 21:52). Congratulations to all those breaking their personal bests, particularly that solid and well-populated brass section.

The Milestones

Shepton Mallet folk wizards, The Milestones, were booked for the difficult mid-festival set but only singer-songwriter Craig Drew (25:38) showed up for his 25th parkrun. Rumours are that he's thinking of pursuing a rewarding solo career in parkrun.

The First-timers

Underground punk anarchists new not just to Street, but to parkrun. Bass player Kat Powell kept up a superb pace on the strings to record a very respectable 28:49, not bad for a first go at parkrun. On drums Paul Martin maintained a staccato rhythm for a brisk 22:49. A mosh pit formed with the electric energy the band generated. I found myself drawn in for a sweaty 28:54, my fastest parkrun since March 2020. The road back from injury and COVID has been hard but progress is being made in the spirit of punk defiance.

The Torists

This bunch of intrepid didgeridoo and throat-singing musicians travelled from far and wide to obtain their parkrun kicks. They particularly like to perform in Glastonbury during the May Day celebrations. We had travellers from Chester and Essex today, but no Australians.

Anita Forsyth and the Tail Walkers

After a brief pause for changeover of running gear between sets, there was a riotous performance from the joyous jazz ensemble, Anita Forsyth and the Tail Walkers. Anita laid down one of the fastest final times I've seen in parkrun (37:37).

The Cowbell Crew

Headlining this morning were the stalwart new wave legends, The Cowbell Crew. Without the 19 volunteers the festival of running at Street would not happen on a weekly basis. Their music is more concept album than chart hit but the enthusiasm of the volunteers makes sure you have a great start to the day. Keep a look out for musical lyricist Tim Rice marshalling on the approach to Street Summit, cowbell ringing like Ski Sunday!

26. HUMBER BRIDGE

Run Report: Larkin around the Alps, 14/05/2022

A trip with friends to the Lincolnshire Wolds, staying in the wonderfully named Old Ice Cream Shop, meant a visit to Humber Bridge parkrun. Having already run the charming Market Rasen Racecourse, a tourist streak necessitated hitting the north for a run in what they call Little Switzerland! The country park at Humber Bridge is so-called because the chalk cliffs resemble the snow-covered peaks of the Alps. The north face of the Eiger might be appropriate for one or two of the cliffs and for the undulating nature of the course! With the Alpine connotation, here is the parkrun today told through the 8 stages of mountaineering for unfit people I found online:

Stage 1: Excitement

It's hard to deny the excitement of Humber Bridge parkrun is raised by a drive over the suspension bridge coming up from North Lincolnshire. The reality of the run is yet to sink in. Anything was possible for the 122 athletes looked after by 15 Eiger volunteers.

Stage 2: Optimism

After the run briefing, there's the optimism of the first mile. If you're lucky heavy breathing has not set in and you feel like you're on for a personal best. This is the most dangerous part of the parkrun.

Stage 3: Shock and denial

And then it hits just after the first mile. The pace slows and the breathing resembles Darth Vader or Michael Myers after a hundred metre sprint. The energy suddenly disappears from the legs on lap two of the circuit of the country park as the topographic undulation bites. You're not enjoying those sheer cliffs any longer.

Stage 4: Anger and bargaining

Around halfway, you check your watch. The pace has definitely slowed but you're three seconds ahead of where you need to be. In your mind, you can still do this. The rage inside your legs says otherwise. This stage does not apply to first finishers John Riddiough (16:58) and Jennifer Smith (24:40).

Stage 5: Working through and acceptance

By the start of the third mile, whatever will be will be. You're now a minute off where you had hoped to be due to a woeful lack of training as the great fade has got you in its grip. Luckily, the cheery marshals help you realise that a run is just a run. And that Humber Bridge Country Park is a fine place to run, one of the top woodland runs.

Stage 6: Elation

Crashing into the finish funnel it takes at least two minutes for you to be able to speak again after a sprint that felt like Usain Bolt but was probably more like the Marshmallow Man after a heavy night on the juice. Having missed your PB by well over a minute, the elation is purely from the runner's high and the satisfaction that another parkrun has been completed, in this case my 77th different global one. David Munday travelled from Manchester for his 108th different event. Dave Monaghan racked up his 250th parkrun to earn the coveted green milestone t-shirt while Mark A Hunt ran his 100th parkrun for the black vest. My friends Nick Harpur and Julie Cooley completed their 'difficult' second parkruns in the shadow of the Humber Bridge dodging the tree roots and steps. It was Mary Pratt's birthday and the chocolates were enjoyed by all, especially the 16 athletes who recorded a new course PB.

Stage 7: Surrender

Having reached the finish it dawns on you that you're parkrun fresh for the whole day and that only half of the challenge has been completed. Unworried you surrender to the stench, safe in the knowledge that everyone will know what you've been up to in your running gear.

Stage 8: Hangover

You swear never again. No more parkruns. No more travelling over four hours for a parkrun. Welcome to the land of the lay in on Saturday mornings. Sadly, everyone knows you'll be there at 9 am next week for the same punishment. It's an addiction from which there is no cure.

Tim's Tourist Tip-off

On the road to Hull, Hessle is the home (253 Hull Road, Hessle) to Philip Larkin's first publishers, George and Jean Hartley.

Larkin (1922-1985) is one of my favourite poets, being responsible for some of the 20th century's finest poetry. He worked for a long time as a librarian at the University of Hull. Why not walk some of the Larkin Trail which stretches along the Humber Estuary in the East Riding of Yorkshire? You'll visit Hull and the desolate peninsula of Spurn Head further to the east where you are exposed to the vast expanse of the North Sea. On our visit there, we found the 3.5 mile walk to Spurn Point a superb one for finding seagrass (there's an eelgrass restoration area) on the shore and for views of the large ships which enter the Humber. Watch out for the hordes of brown-tail moth caterpillars with their irritant hairs and don't get cut off by the high tide.

Poetry Corner

No run report on the Larkin Trail would be complete without sharing one of Philip Larkin's poems that could easily apply to parkrun. 'Days' is a short poem written in 1953 and published in his seminal collection 'The Whitsun Weddings' in 1964. Enjoy.

Days

What are days for?
Days are where we live.
They come, they wake us
Time and time over.
They are to be happy in:
Where can we live but days?

Ah, solving that question
Brings the priest and the doctor
In their long coats
Running over the fields.

Philip Larkin

The wait at Humber Bridge

27. PEEL

Run Report: Stop me if you think you've heard this run before, 28/05/2022

Madchester parkrun hits (available on vinyl only)

I had to travel to Peel parkrun at some point. Many of my favourite bands come from the Manchester area: A Certain Ratio, Buzzcocks, Happy Mondays, James, Joy Division, The Chameleons, The Charlatans, The Fall, The Smiths and The Stone Roses. Music journalist and musician John Robb, frontman of legendary post-punk band the Membranes (a favourite of John Peel), is no stranger to the importance of Manchester for alternative rock having spent much of the 1980s gigging on the scene with the band. He's written popular books on Nirvana and The Stone Roses, edits punk zine Louder Than War and "runs in Peel Park sometimes" when he's in the city. Robb is punk to the core. What greater endorsement does Peel Park need for a run? The pleasantly warm and sunny morning (apparently unusual for Manchester!) was perfect for the 78th different global location on my parkrun poet travels. Let's drop the needle on the record without further delay…

Flood will tear us apart (Joy Division)

Peel Park is situated on the River Irwell floodplain in Salford. It was opened in 1846 and named after Sir Robert Peel, the then Prime Minister. It has the distinction of possibly being the first urban park to be opened anywhere in the world. The fame of Peel Park was further enhanced by a visit from Queen Victoria in 1851 and several paintings by renowned Salford artist L.S. Lowry. In 1861 the Irwell flooded the area causing widespread devastation and several deaths. The granite obelisk near the start was erected in 1867 to mark the flood level.

This is the run (The Stone Roses)

The course is a simple two lapper starting at the statue before athletes drop down onto the concrete riverside path. I counted three shopping trolleys in the river. That is enough excitement for any parkrun. Then comes the Salford South Face, a gentle uphill slope onto the grassy football pitch before you meander back through the shade of trees to the start/finish area for the second lap.

Second skin (The Chameleons)

The difficult second lap takes in a higher path along the River Irwell, negating the need for a calf curdling second ascent of Salford South Face. It's flat and fast so go for it, this is a PB course. The Chameleons are also my favourite band. Go check them out!

Hit the north (The Fall)

I came from Manningtree in north Essex. I needed little excuse to travel far for my first parkrun in the north-west. We also had tourists from Denmark (Janus Boye), Leek (John Forrester) and Rochdale (the Sconer's Running Club). The runner's high meant we were all totally wired.

I know it's over (The Smiths)

For event 34 we had 326 finishers supported by a legion of Lowry-esque marshals (in reality 24 Salford supernovas).

Step on (Happy Rundays)

Twisting their melons hard, first finishers Louis Szymanski (16:57) and Leona Beaumont (21:39) proved they did not suffer from lazyitis as I do. Hallelujah with a Bez-style dance and clack of the castanets overlaid by the soulful vocals of Rowetta.

Please, please, please, let me get the PB I want (The Smiths)

For (at least!) once in their lives, an incredible 88 athletes (27% of field) got what they wanted with new course PBs. Heaven knows we also had 7 Smiths running and an Ian Brown!

24 minute parkrun people (Happy Rundays)

For no other reason than I've never quite managed it (PB 25:12), let's celebrate the 110 athletes who ran the hallowed sub-25 min parkrun. Let me know how it feels sometime.

The only run I know (The Charlatans)

Some 20 runners are not charlatans. They've been bathed in the warm light of parkrun and completed their first run. Go forth and conquer. There is a light that never goes out. If you find it, let me know.

Ever fallen in love (with parkrun you shouldn't have) (Buzzcocks)

We all know parkrun is addictive. Hell, I'd driven 250 miles to run 3.1! Also under the spell of parkrun are Andrea Keeler (25 Club), Adam Smith (50 Club), Andy Thomas (100 Club) and Joe Smith (150 parkruns). Two 500 Clubbers ran as well (Chris and Liz Jones).

Tim's Tourist Tip-off

After Peel parkrun it's an embarrassment of riches for things to do although the Joy Division-inspired café Atmosphere was shut post-run. If you're making a weekend of it the parkrun is near to the Salford Museum and Art Gallery which has a replica Victorian street and is free! I decided to pay a pilgrimage to nearby Salford Lads' Club (opened in 1903) which features in a music video by The Smiths and on the sleeve of The Queen Is Dead, a classic album from the Mancunian melancholics. After the obligatory photo outside from character-laden Coronation Street, it's free to enter on Saturdays. The listed building is Tardis-like in that it's much larger inside than it looks from the road. The Salford Lads' Club includes a Smiths' room, boxing ring and gym. Salford lad Eddie Colman was a member of the club football team before progressing on to Manchester United (108 appearances). He was tragically killed in the Munich air disaster of 1958 at the age of just 21. He is remembered here.

Poetry Corner

I ran in a Jog Division running vest and had hoped to swing a few gladioli in homage to Morrissey, lead singer of The Smiths, who performed with these flowers on occasion. Sadly, and perhaps for the best, I couldn't get hold of any! Fortunately, the roadside verges and roundabouts were resplendent with wildflowers and pollinators benefitting from No Mow May, very heartening to see for a bumblebee researcher like me and appropriate given that the worker bee is the symbol of Manchester. The following short haiku-like poems are inspired by Peel Park, the Manchester scene and Salford Lads' Club:

cornflower
the worker bee
hasn't forgotten you

post-modern
Lowry figures run

for the old
personal best
flood obelisk

THAT bandstand
will see me out

through a narrow door
a large welcome

fresh shadows
on boxing ring canvas

After parkrun visit for fans of The Smiths!

28. RENDLESHAM FOREST

Run Report: In spruce, no-one can hear you scream, 04/06/2022

Aliens return for the Jubilee!

Warp drive disengaged. Cruising speed at an altitude of 5 kilometres. We're somewhere over the south-east coast of England. Apparently, it's The Festival of Suffolk today to mark the Platinum Jubilee of Queen Elizabeth II (reign 70 years). There should be a good turnout of runners and walkers for what is known as parkrun on earth. Parkrun is a weekly, timed, free event initiated in 2004 to improve the fitness and community spirit of *Homo sapiens*. It's a great idea. I'm not sure why we have nothing like it at home on Titan, one of Saturn's moons? The Titans would love it, energetic bunch of three-legged sentient beings that they are. Parkrun seems so much more suited to the beginner than the ultra-marathon around Saturn's A ring (169,943 miles or 273,496 kilometres). We've seen things you people wouldn't believe.

The location appears as we remember from those fateful nights in December 1980 when we buzzed the clearing in Rendlesham Forest. That was such fun. And it created hysteria in human society. They've even installed a fake UFO on an alien trail through the conifer trees. They were so close to making first contact and now some think it was a hoax! Cue maniacal Titan laughter. It is out of this world.

We've been receiving radio signals for years from parkrun event teams to extract the parkrun poet Tim Gardiner for crimes against poetry and running. It will have to be a low-key abduction with standard beam take-up, which shouldn't pose a problem as he's towards the back of the pack these days. Today, he's dressed up in some ridiculous red, white and blue Stormtrooper get up from the popular movie franchise, Star Wars. Cue more diabolical Titan laughter. He will enjoy meeting our pet xenomorph!

To begin with parkrunners gather for some kind of briefing from their leader (top earthling Clive Shaw). It appears to go well with lots of clapping and copious mentions of the dangers of tree roots and pine cones falling on heads. There is plenty of colour out there, red, white and blue abounds to mark the Platinum Jubilee. There are 22 marshals in high visibility jackets with walkie talkie radios. One almost spots us hovering lower over the trees as the morning sun glints off our metal craft and they radio someone. We must switch to cloaking mode to avoid further alarm.

At 09:00 hours, the runners and walkers are off, snaking along narrow tracks through pine trees. Our scanner detects 107 humans participating along with several dogs. The course is a one-lap affair of sandy paths and undulations. Parkrunners climb steadily up a sandy hill halfway to the flat summit (let's call it UFO Plateau!) where we were 'seen' all those years ago by personnel from the US airbase! The parkrun poet trips on a tree root, clearly ignoring the advice from the run briefing, and falls for the fourth time in over 100 parkruns! What a clumsy fool! In true parkrun fashion, he is helped up by a fellow runner.

It's the perfect trail run for those who love a forest moon. Humans are also pretty quick for bipeds. Tom Fairbrother (setting a new course record of 16:52) and Sophie Rose (22:47) hit the funnel with blistering pace. I think our three-legged Titans may be more suited to the longer distance ultras around Saturn's rings than this sprint fest.

They celebrate milestones on earth. Victoria Tapp completed her 50th parkrun to earn the coveted scarlet running vest. The parkrun poet's son, tourist Joseph Gardiner, completed his 30th different parkrun to enter the global Most Events list. Seven people were new to parkrun completing their first run. Thirteen humanoids recorded a course PB.

Due to the Jubilee weekend, people had travelled to run at the site of Britain's Roswell (aren't humans laughable with their imaginations?) from Cambridge, Derbyshire, Hertfordshire, London, Southend and Worcester. They were able to feast on some delicious cakes after the run kindly provided by volunteers to celebrate the Jubilee and The Festival of Suffolk. Due to the parkrun poet's son being present we're not able to take him up this time. We need the poet alone. We will return earthlings. This is not over; you will be free of poetry. We will speak to parkrun HQ about setting up zero gravity events on Titan! Warp drive engaged.

The Titans' Tourist Tip-off

There is no need to leave the Tangham area of Rendlesham Forest for your post-parkrun entertainment. Follow the UFO trail from the car park and discover the story behind Britain's Roswell. It's a pleasant 5K loop that will take in the distinctive 'life size' UFO sculpture on the other side of Rendlesham Forest. There are interpretation boards along the route that tell our story. Did we visit Rendlesham Forest in December 1980? You decide!

Poetry Corner

We leave you with four short haiku-like poems which highlight the original sightings in 1980. From confusion with Orford Lighthouse, fireballs, animals driven crazy to motivations for an alien visitation, read on:

>lighthouse
>again and again
>the truth

>the muntjac's bark
>no hoax

>fireball
>oh look!
>trail of ice cream

>earth's a long detour
>ask yourself why

Imperial trooper 'charge' at Rendlesham Forest
© Rendlesham Forest parkrun

Three peaks of Eildon Hill can be seen from Wallaceneuk

29. WALLACENEUK

Run Report: They have brought you to the run, now dance if you can, 11/06/2022

sharing

another secret –

unfolding buds

Haiku from Edinburgh poet, Juliet Wilson, that easily applies to Wallaceneuk parkrun.

It's been far too long, but I'm back in Kelso at the confluence of the Tweed and Teviot. I love this big country with its hillsides of bilberry, gorse and heather. This morning we gather for the 50th parkrun celebrations at Wallaceneuk. We have 80 athletes and 17 stoical volunteers prepared to brave the windy and cool weather. The wind does at least keep the midges away! Several Cub Scouts are running or walking the course and there's cakes after the parkrun. Someone has travelled up from Worcester, while that tedious typist and parkrun poet (Tim Gardiner) is here all the way from Essex.

The town's representative known as Kelso Laddie (Callum Davidson for 2022) is here to start the parkrun to celebrate Kelso Civic Week. The Kelso Laddie tradition began in 1937 and has returned after a two-year absence due to the pandemic. There are plenty of Kelso Civic Week goodies to be given away as prizes including baseball caps and rosettes. Turning away to look at the mound covered in ox-eye daisy flowers, I spot a red deer stag among the bushes on the far side of the clearing. Its gaze is fixed on me, its body unflinching. The stag is not even bothered by the assembled parkrunners. Eventually, it retreats into dense foliage.

After run director Michael Lewis's witty briefing, Kelso Laddie starts the parkrun. Runners and walkers file down the hill onto the railway path which runs for a mile and a half to the triangular turnaround area just before the viaduct at Roxburgh. On the outward section there are terrific views of the three-peaks of Eildon Hill if you look to the right in open sections and a yellow banquet of bird's-foot trefoil lining the path. I feel the presence of the unseen stag running through the trees. Somehow our fates seem intertwined and ancient like distant Eildon Hill. After the turnaround, the stag is leading me along the railway line as if spurred on by the malevolence of some unseen force. The mist doesn't know our breath nor the wind or rain. Neither of us can rest.

There is a gentle slope to the homeward section before the short but sharp hill preceding the finish funnel which is perfect for finishing off any runner or walker! The observant parkrunner will have noticed Floors Castle to the left before the hill. First finishers Darrell Hastie (16:25) and Sophie Horrocks (19:58) record scorching times for this challenging trail run, the former a new course record to celebrate the 50th event. Milestones this morning include John Dryburgh's 150th parkrun and Jasper Harrison's 10th Junior parkrun (JM11-14) for which he earns the white running vest.

The parkrun poet was here for his second Scottish parkrun, recording a new parkrun PB for Scotland of 30:20 after a tough inauguration at ultra-hilly Ganavan Sands in summer 2021 (33:47). I'm not sure he's seen the deer or whether he even can. Not yet. I cannot stay long in human company. The stag is calling me. I must run with him across the viaduct to Wallace's Tower and beyond to the sandstone statue.

Tim's Tourist Tip-off

The Kelso area is known for its historical significance and natural beauty. The ruins of Roxburgh Castle are found at the junction of the Tweed and Teviot on a windswept hilltop and can be seen from the A699. The castle was often in English hands during the First War of Scottish Independence (1296-1328) before being retaken by the Scots in 1314. In modern Roxburgh, you can see Wallace's Tower in a field near the viaduct, although it's believed that its name is unrelated to the warrior William Wallace who fought in the area before his execution in 1305.

A few miles to the west of Kelso, the first statue of Wallace to be erected (in 1814) can be visited at Melrose. The red sandstone statue overlooks the stunning peaks of Eildon Hill and is near Scott's View which is associated with Scottish writer Sir Walter Scott, author of Rob Roy published in 1817. Why not take a walk on Eildon Hill which Stuart Adamson wrote about (in the superb song Eiledon from 1986) with his seminal Scottish rock band Big Country. Walter Scott was similarly inspired almost two centuries before with his 1805 poem The Lay of the Last Minstrel which suggests that King Arthur's everlasting sleep is in a cave beneath the hill. Eildon Hill has three summits (some say four, there is a wee crag!).

As you can see the three summits from Wallaceneuk, why not complete the Eildon Three Peaks after the parkrun? Simply trek up all three summits of Eildon Hill (1700 feet of elevation gain) and finish the parkrun to complete the challenge. The three peaks are (and best summited in this order): North Hill (404 m above sea level), Mid Hill (422 m) and Wester Hill (371 m) while the unofficial Little Hill is a short diversion from the route for the completists.

Poetry Corner

I finish with a sequence of short haiku-like poems inspired by the parkrun and the surrounding landscape:

nettles
castle ruins
under new management

wildcat
when will you rebel

rise up
with the deer stag
and run

where hills meet sky
rainbow long gone

with the wind
to Wallace's Tower
curlew cry
distant hill
born again at sunrise

30. ALTON WATER

Run Report: Pulp Friction, 18/06/2022

There's already been a Reservoir Jog podcast by top tourist and With Me Now legend Danny Norman, so here is the Tarantino follow up parkrun movie. Pulp Friction is a parkrun tale told in a non-linear fashion of seven parts like the film!

1. Prologue: the cafe. Two volunteers sit deep in conversation, often heated at times. They're not sure what happened to the missing tokens. Decided on the course of action, they stand up and announce to the café that they require every last finish token that wasn't dropped in the scanner's bucket!

2. Prelude to the parkrun. Sometime earlier, 63 athletes turned up for the parkrun looked after superbly by 12 volunteers. Highland Cows with their shaggy brown coats observed from behind the fence, grazing the dam banks to maintain the diversity of wildflowers in the grassland. Maddy Barrett gave an enthusiastic first-timers' briefing before run director Matt Thompson delivered the run briefing ensuring we were off at 9 am without delay.

3. The mooshals. The Highland Cows acted as the unofficial marshals (mooshals?!) along the course, a two-lap perambulation of the attractive west side of the 160 ha reservoir that supplies water to the Ipswich and Felixstowe areas of south Suffolk. The perimeter of the reservoir is 13 km (8 miles), a run I've done several times in preparation for longer runs. Alton Water parkrun is an undulating course like much of the trail around the reservoir. The parkrun has fine views of Alton Water and the distant belltower of the Royal Hospital School which looms on

the horizon like one of Tolkien's towers! There is a short section of wooded path to the north of the lap before you drop down the reservoir bank to run alongside the water towards the start and finish area.

4. Prelude to the timekeeper's watch. This morning we had a tourist from Norfolk (Sarah Lake) completing her 73rd different parkrun location while Tony Liddell ran at his 115th different parkrun. It was my 81st different global location on the parkrun poetry tour which has taken me to Japan, Scotland and Wales. There were no milestones this morning but it was encouraging to see 10 athletes new to parkrun including three members of the Bond family. Shaken, not stirred!

5. The timekeeper's watch. Today's timelords, Maddy Barrett and Joseph Thompson, watches calibrated with the Royal Hospital School belltower of course, clocked first finishers Andrew Farn at 19:18 and Gemma Moss at 25:51. There were also six course PBs this morning, well done to all.

6. The poetry situation. I wasn't feeling particularly poetic in the summer heat but did manage to find inspiration in the natural surroundings of the reservoir and the far-off views of the belltower across the water. However, I didn't hear its chimes at 9:15 am and 9:30 am over my heavy breathing!

7. Epilogue: the café. Frazzled from the warm sun and undulating parkrun my son Joseph and I went prospecting for pastries in the café by the car park. Two volunteers are sat deep in conversation near the door. They appear to be clean out of five-dollar shakes and only accept Sterling. The panoramic vista of the reservoir was ample compensation though. Joseph admits that Alton Water is a fine venue for a parkrun and adds another scenic trail run (along with fellow recent addition Rendlesham

Forest) to the collection of Suffolk parkruns, known as Suff-ok when all locations are completed. Once all parkrun locations in Norfolk and Suffolk have been run or walked it's known as That's All Folks and the wider East Anglia challenge (Norfolk, Suffolk and Cambridgeshire) is East Ran-glia! As Joseph goes to the toilet, the two volunteers stand up and loudly ask where the missing finishing tokens are…

Tim's Tourist Tip-off

There is much to enjoy at Alton Water itself. You can take a 1.5 mile walk north along the track used by the parkrun towards the Tattingstone Wonder, a folly which was initially two cottages. Edward White, a local squire, added a third cottage because he didn't like the view of it from his property at Tattingstone Place in 1790. To complete the transformation he added a fake church tower and flint façade. Truly unique and worth the short wander. If you're still feeling energetic after the parkrun, why not run around the reservoir, an 8 mile loop. Be warned though that the path is the definition of undulating although the views are adequate payback.

Along the B1080, the impressive belltower of the Royal Hospital School can be viewed at closer range, a distinctive feature of the horizon from the parkrun course. The belltower is best seen from Lower Holbrook (a small, free car park is available), a vast tidal bay with walks along the seawall and shoreline towards Harkstead. There are impressive crag cliffs (look out for sharks' teeth) and plenty of salt marsh and seagrass on the beach and mudflats where coastal birds are plentiful.

Poetry Corner

To follow up last week's haiku poems from my trip to Wallaceneuk parkrun in the Scottish Borders, here are two short haiku-like poems inspired by the parkrun:

> bell chime
> clearest on
> a dawn breeze

> thunder of feet
> the cow's alarm call

Highland Cows at Alton Water

31. DARLINGTON SOUTH PARK

Run Report: While my Garmin gently weeps, 25/06/2022

My visit to Darlington from the south coincided with Global Beatles Day. So naturally, I'm dropping the needle on the greatest hits of the Beatles to tell the tale of Event 423:

Come together

On a breezy, yet sunny morning in South Park we had 306 parkrunners supported by 23 volunteers. For my first parkrun in the north-east, I was made to feel more than welcome. As a solo tourist to most parkruns, it's great to talk to other parkrunners and volunteers before and after the run to soak in the community atmosphere.

Yesterday

….all my troubles seemed so far away. Writing this report back in Essex on a quiet Sunday morning, part of me wishes I was still in South Park. It's one of the finest parks I've visited with an aviary, bandstand, clock tower, lake, rose garden (I never promised you one!), River Skerne and two towering giant redwood trees planted in 1863. A parrot known as Max used to live in the aviary and would shout obscenities (f-word) at people passing by making him a local celebrity. Sadly, Max died in 2014 otherwise he would've been one hell of a marshal!

The fool on the hill

I was forewarned by prolific parkrun tourist, Helen Rutter, herself from the north-east, about the infamous Squirrel Hill. Of course, having run many undulating trail parkruns, I scoffed at the potential challenge! How bad could it be? After a lovely 'sprint' from the start and a downhill dash, the short and sharp hill before the start and finish area is a shock to the system on the second and third laps! After the initial steep slope (c. 9% gradient), the hill has a sting in the tail as the path doesn't really flatten out until a little way past the old fountain. Fair wind to the finish after that!

Rubber sole (entire album)

The quicksters today were Michael Joyeux (17:00) and Felicity Hannon (19:08). Peace and love were supplied by tail-walker Anne Reidy. I should also mention the polite parkrunner, Steve McAllister, who apologised to me as he buried me in the sprint finish. It's this dry humour and spirit that keeps me coming back to parkrun week after week.

Day trippers

There were a variety of parkrunners who'd travelled for the experience from as far away as Clapham, Essex (not the same as London!) and Newcastle.

I saw him standing there

There are few parkruns that have a time-keeper mid-lap so to see Harbhag Singh near the bandstand providing time updates was a lovely touch. His prophesy on lap 3 that I'd run 29:40 was pretty accurate (29:43).

The long and winding road

Getting fitter and quicker at parkrun requires long-term commitment. It'll be a bumpy road with many twists and turns as form comes and goes. Congratulations to Clare Murray, Dean Standish and Nathalie Paxton who reached the 25 Milestone Club with their runs. It's a solid start to a long and winding road, one that rewards persistence.

Let it PB

Sing along to this classic for the 40 parkrunners who achieved a new course PB this morning.

When I'm sixty-four

Most annoyingly, there were no runners or walkers who completed their 64th parkrun.

Tomorrow never knows

Hopefully, the journey will continue for the 12 parkrunners who completed their first parkrun. The 'difficult' second parkrun beckons!

Strawberry scones forever

After the exhaustion of Squirrel Hill, thrice climbed, the scones in the café near Clock Tower Lodge were delicious.

Tim's Tourist Tip-off

There is no need to move too far from South Park for post-parkrun entertainment for those making a day or weekend of it. The park itself is a relaxing place to explore with the lake, wood areas, the undulation between high and low parts and the rose garden. For those wanting to explore the Skerne Valley, a left turn at the bottom of Squirrel Hill and through the gate under the road, leads to a pleasant walk along the river. It's a short walk through the flood meadows to the fishing lake near the A66 where you'll see an abundance of butterflies such as the meadow brown and ringlet in summer along with dragonflies hawking among the reeds.

Poetry Corner

Following last week's haiku poems from my trip to Alton Water parkrun in Suffolk, here are two short haiku-like poems inspired by the parkrun:

>giant redwoods
>clock tower
>know your place

>in rose garden shade
>no lovers

32. EDINBURGH

Run Report: Run away aft with ye! 09/07/2022

Here's a run report through the eyes of fictional characters created by Edinburgh's own Robert Louis Stevenson. My dad instilled a love of adventure with his enthusiastic readings of Treasure Island and Kidnapped when I was a child. This report also owes its inspiration to top parkrun tourist John Buchanan who went to the same school as Stevenson.

Benn Gunn (Treasure Island)

Cramond Island used to be a peaceful place to hide away from people. But since that darn causeway was built, there's been no end of visitors at low tide. This morning I'm rudely awakened by another rave, making getting back to sleep impossible. I've grown tired of scaring the ravers away with my ghostly voice, it doesn't work so well in a digital age of scepticism. To get away from the monotonous racket, I row over to the mainland.

Safely moored, I see 24 volunteers setting up for a crowd of 344 parkrunners (I count people as quick as pieces of eight!). I can't run or walk the necessary 5 km these days, my dodgy knees prevent that. I could be a useful marshal though, giving spiritual encouragement from the bushes along the promenade. It's an out and back course so I'll get to scare the runners and walkers twice. Due to the linear and straight-forward nature of the route, a few carefully positioned skeletons laid out pointing the way should do the directional job for athletes.

David Balfour (Kidnapped)

I'm early for the parkrun, having travelled from Appin on the west coast. I notice an odd man disappear into the bushes which reminds me of the murder of the Red Fox. Staying out of the bushman's sight, for worry he may be another Red Fox murdering sniper, I watch the run briefing enthusiastically delivered by a fashionably late Andrew Burnie set to the distant thunder of the Cramond Island rave. Milestones are announced: Arthur Crummie and David Keiller are completing their 50th run. We have tourists from the Derwent Valley and Rutland. There are also tourists from Essex including the parkrun poet, Tim Gardiner, who looks dangerously out of shape to be honest despite this being his 83rd different global parkrun location and 124th run in all. He'll struggle with the headwind on the return section, that's if the midges haven't seen to him before then. A bizarre fellow comes up to me and asks if I'm also a parkrun tourist. He's from London you see. The strange man is focused on the run and not at all relaxed. With the guy in the bush and this character hanging around, I decide to leave and collect my fortune from Uncle Ebenezer at the House of Shaws in Cramond. I hear he has a blunderbuss!

Dr. Jekyll

After young David has wandered off in the direction of the House of Shaws, I ready myself for the big test. I'm hoping for a new parkrun PB this morning. After the off, I rattle along the promenade passing fenced off areas of planted wildflowers to encourage pollinators and a greening the grey seawall section where textured surfaces have been installed on tidal concrete walls to persuade sea creatures to colonise. I'm trying to keep up with the other runners but it's hard work; increasingly my breathing becomes laboured and the head slumps. I'd promised myself not to use the serum, but at the turnaround I take a swig from the small bottle to help with the headwind.

Mr. Hyde and the nuns

A manic energy infuses my running. The pace picks up noticeably into the headwind as I see the far off Forth Bridge loom into view. I pass fading runners including the parkrun poet with ease. Sadly, I've left it far too late with the potion to catch the first finishers. An abusive idiot hidden in a bush further enrages me near the finish as I flick another midge off my face. The unseen clown in the trees makes one quip too many and I duck out of the funnel and chase the comedian along the prom passing a group of nuns on a day out! In time, I lose sight of the hilarious heckler and flop onto a patch of grass exhausted, the serum finally worn off. I receive some funny looks off the meandering nuns. I'm woken by Edinburgh parkrun stalwart Chris Pilley who's run over 400 times on the course and wondered if I was alright having seen me haring around after the noisy deviant from the bushes. While I was sleeping the results email came through. The first finishers, Aaron Wilson and Amy Crawford, have impressed with 16:48 and 20:30, respectively, while there were 38 new PBs. Congratulations to all. After this debacle, I'm letting Jekyll run next week….

Sunshine on Keith Award

Keith Burns was the fastest Keith this week with a sprightly 20:17! Sadly, he was the only Keith this morning but that's a very quick time none-the-less. The Keith course record was set by Keith Hood with a blistering 15:58 on 10th August 2013.

Tim's Tourist Tip-off

Where do you start for post-parkrun sight-seeing in Edinburgh? There's the famous castle nestled high on the precipice of Castle Rock and the popular Calton Hill with its observatory and tower. Arthur's Seat in Holyrood Park is well worth the walk or run to admire the panoramic views of the city. Legend suggests that the hill was the site of the mythical Camelot. At low tide a walk across the causeway near the parkrun start to Cramond Island is an unmissable experience. The causeway is lined with pyramidal stones which were a defence against German U-boats in World War II. Across the river towards the Forth Bridge is an extension of Drum Sands which can be accessed via the John Muir Way. Here you will see Eagle Rock and Barnbougle Castle across the cockled bay. There are large meadows of seagrass here, the dark green leaves of which can be viewed laying prostrate on the mudflats at low tide. Seagrass is important as habitat for fish and seahorses, for carbon sequestration and also in protecting coastal areas from the erosive effects of wave action. Seagrass has declined greatly in the UK in the last few decades with up to 98% of meadows lost in some areas. Seagrass can be found near other coastal parkruns including Scotland's Ganavan Sands and Chalkwell Beach in Essex along the Thames Estuary.

Poetry Corner

For the second time in one of my parkrun reports, I include a three-line haiku (old maps, first published in Femku magazine, Issue 31, Nov 2022) from renowned Edinburgh poet, Juliet Wilson, followed by a two-line haiku poem of mine inspired by the parkrun:

old maps
where now
are all those trees

only one winner, crab
causeway tide

Nuns on the run at Edinburgh

33. PEGWELL BAY

Run Report: Ring of firebugs! 16/07/2022

By a fictional down on his luck smuggler of souvenirs

I've messed up again! Last night's flashing light from the clifftop directed me further east than the old hoverport into the seaweed tunnel. Smuggling isn't what it used to be; you just can't get reliable look-out light operatives anymore. The contraband of old is replaced by cheap tack and souvenirs for the seafront shops in Ramsgate. Hauling the cargo of Viking helmets out of the boat, I notice some tiny red and black bugs at the tunnel entrance. They look like the firebugs you see in France, known as 'Gendarmes' which feed on the seeds of pink flowers such as mallow which are abundant in the Pegwell Bay area.

Outside of the seaweed tunnel the dawn sky is cloudless, it's going to be a hot one. Pegwell Bay is as picturesque as I remember with chalk cliffs, salt marsh and mudflats. Leaving the contraband and its firebugs until dusk to move, I decide to spend the morning at the nearby parkrun. I follow a meandering path up the chalk cliffs to a large ship. It's a replica Scandinavian longboat (named Hugin) to mark the landing of the Germanic brothers Hengist and Horsa who led the Angles, Saxons and Jutes into Britain over 1500 years ago. They were more successful than Julius Caesar who led two invasions of Britain, probably through Pegwell Bay.

Dodging a couple of mods on a multi-mirrored Vespa, I arrive at Pegwell Bay Country Park for the run briefing just before the parkrun start. People have travelled from as far away as Norway for today's entertainment. It's Pegwell Bay's 407th event and there are 22 superb volunteers here to help with its smooth running. Due to the heat, they have a water station for the second lap with cups of water to keep runners and walkers cool which is a lovely gesture from the volunteers for which all are thankful.

The course is two laps of the Country Park along tarmac and gravel paths with little tree cover so there is no real shade to regulate the temperature of runners and walkers. On the final stretch before the left turn into the start and finish area there are panoramic views of Pegwell Bay and the chalk cliffs near Ramsgate which must surely rank as one of the finest vistas in parkrun-land. In quiet moments, the plaintiff cry of a curlew can be heard along with the 'peep-ing' exclamation of the oystercatcher. In summer, paths are fringed with mallow and clover flowers and insects such as Roesel's bush-cricket buzz from the long grass.

The 123 athletes begin their quest at 9 am sharp. I line up with the marshals giving out cups of water at the start of the second lap. The parkrun poet Tim Gardiner needs a lot of cooling down, he's struggling already! All manner of running vests pass by including Coastal Striders, Dover Road Runners, The Minnis Bay Bees, Salvation Army, Saxon Shore Striders, Thanet Road Runners and Vegan Runners.

It's nice to see the runners come in. This morning, first finishers Mathieu Chavey (17:37) and Annette Shrimpton (21:51) have overcome the hairdryer conditions to record very quick times. The juniors (under 11) also excelled today: Jake Screene (26:49) and Isabella Saxby (27:10) have bright parkrun futures ahead. There are 3 new PBs: Adam Sanderson, Claire London and Clive London. Congratulations to them all. We have 500 club legend David Llewellyn (With Me Now) with us as well as Mark Savage who joins the 50 club, having run all of those at Pegwell Bay.

That's inspirational loyalty! Kirsty McMahon completed her 25th run to earn the coveted first milestone vest.

At the end of the run there's drinks for all taking part which are much needed given the heatwave. The heat. Did I mention the heat?! I slip quietly away back to my stash of helmets to distribute after dark. On the way, I'm nearly run over by a guy on a Lambretta! The mods are out in force today. One asks me what attracts folk to parkrun. I can't explain…I think it's love.

Tim's Tourist Tip-off

You're spoilt for choice in Pegwell Bay. A short walk up to the replica Viking ship is a must followed by an exploration of the old hoverport area which is being reclaimed by nature after it fell into disuse in 1987. It's a derelict wilderness of bramble and buddleia. Some would call it rewilding. A little further along the coast towards Ramsgate is the Seaweed Tunnel which is thought to have been driven through the cliff to provide access to the beach for seaweed collection. The seaweed would then have been used as a fertiliser.

Further east still, firebugs were recorded by the parkrun poet at Western Undercliff Beach at the northern extent of Pegwell Bay and also near Ramsgate Port. They were observed near the pink mallow flowers on which they feed. None were found in the Country Park, although they have been recorded nearby so it's only a matter of time before they are unofficial marshals, similar to Harwich parkrun in Essex. Historically, the firebug was rare in the UK with only one known population in Devon but it's now turning up frequently in the south-east, often near ports, suggesting accidental importation from abroad on ferries and container ships.

Poetry Corner

And finally, a couple of short haiku-like poems to celebrate Pegwell Bay parkrun and the surrounding environment:

hoverport bee
a short flight
skimming waves

chasing the light
tunnel vision

Pegwell Bay

34. MALLING

Run Report: Oceans apart, 23/07/2022

Last weekend, I ran at Pegwell Bay without my son Joseph. He astutely picked up that my modest Kent parkrun PB (29:38) was now faster than his for the garden of England (30:04). Admittedly, his best Kentish time was recorded during the tail-end of Storm Eunice in February 2022 at a sodden and hilly Royal Tunbridge Wells (fab course and volunteers though!) and mine was at the much flatter and drier Pegwell Bay! But still, there is an injustice in the world while father is faster than son, so to Malling we travelled from Essex at the start of the school summer holiday. I was instructed to select a flattish run on which he could annihilate my effort. Malling has been on my list of parkruns to tour for a while, so it made sense and besides, it's only 78 miles from Manningtree in Essex, almost a local one for tourists like us! Despite being gently undulating and only two laps, the other advantage of Malling is there is also some shade from tree cover along the route, important in the current hot spell (more for me than him!).

Malling is an attractive run around the large lake they call The Ocean at Leybourne Lakes Country Park. The site was a sand and gravel works which ceased operations in the 1970s, after which restoration took the form of landscaping and flooding of the pits. Nestled between Snodland and New Hythe in the Medway Valley, Leybourne Lakes is a haven for wildlife including great crested grebes, nightingales, water voles, fish (carp and tench), dragonflies and glow-worms. Glow-worms are beetles and their green glow (a pin prick of light) is a fast-vanishing sight in our countryside. Having said this, many parkrun courses have them glowing on summer evenings too: Clare Castle (Suffolk), Coldham's Common (Cambs), Hadleigh

(Essex), Rendlesham Forest (Suffolk) and Sizewell (Suffolk). Leybourne Lakes also has a diverse range of butterflies. The details of Event 264 are relayed through some of the butterflies found at Leybourne Lakes to celebrate the Big Butterfly Count:

Peacock

The peacock is a well-loved butterfly with beautiful eye-spots on the wings. A showy species, much like the 19 fabulous volunteers, several sweltering in high vis jackets.

Large skipper

A lovely orange and brown summer butterfly which flits along hedgerows and through meadows much like our first finishers Matthew Harvey (17:52) and Isobel Seabrook (22:39).

Gatekeeper

Another orange and brown butterfly seen in the Leybourne Lakes meadows or along woodland edge. The gatekeepers of the parkrun times (otherwise known as time lords) ensured that 15 PBs were accurately recorded.

Red admiral

A migrant species. Tourists to Malling included runners from Bournemouth, Essex, Rotterdam and Washington, D.C. That's a decent spread!

Ringlet

This dark brown butterfly has attractive rings on its wings. These could be symbolic of the parkrunners who've completed many laps of Malling and other parkrun events to achieve their milestones. Robert Briggs and Catriona Stringer ran their 25th parkrun to earn their first milestone vest. Congratulations to them!

Small tortoiseshell

This multi-coloured butterfly is frequently found at Leybourne Lakes and is probably spotted in many parkrunners' gardens. It's leading the way for the pint-sized junior parkrunners. This includes my 12-year-old son Joseph who did indeed smash my Kent PB out of the parkrun with 25:06. Order has been restored to our parkrunworld. He's gunning for my Scottish parkrun PB too in a week's time; will he leave me any scraps from the table?

Comma

The comma marks on the wings of this orange butterfly hint at a new and uncertain journey for those folk undertaking their first parkrun. We had 8 runners brand new to parkrun today. Will they complete their 'difficult' second run next week? Let's hope so.

Tim's Tourist Tip-off – St. Leonard's Tower

After a game of spot the oast house (conical hop drying buildings), why not check out West Malling, a market town near Leybourne Lakes. St. Leonard's Tower is a possible Norman keep built by Gundulf, Bishop of Rochester, between 1077 and 1108. It was originally around 22 m tall but was damaged during the English Civil War. Over the years, St. Leonard's Tower has been used for drying (kilning) hops in much the same way as an oast house. A large brass key went missing in 1973 and was returned in 2020 by post with an apology for the delay!

Poetry Corner

Inspired by the circuitous parkrun and its gorgeous natural surroundings, I finish with two short, haiku-like poems:

butterfly

appreciate the shade

its undulations

the gentlest of breezes

tests a mayfly's patience

35. CASSIOBURY

Run Report: Watford – the place is full of pacers!
30/07/2022

My knowledge of Watford comes primarily from the film Daleks' Invasion Earth 2150 A.D. (1966) in which Dr. Who notes "We'll have to bypass Watford. The place is full of Daleks!" Cassiobury Park is no stranger to science fiction films either. Whippendell Wood was used for a forest scene featuring Liam Neeson in Star Wars: Episode 1 – The Phantom Menace. Watford is also home to one of the parkrun poet's favourite post-punk bands – Sad Lovers and Giants – who wrote, with no small measure of melancholy in their jangly guitar style, about local places (Clocktower Lodge). So, with expectations high, I travelled to Cassiobury Park from Essex for different global parkrun number 86 and my 127th run overall. The parkrun looked like it had plenty of tree cover providing shade for runners and walkers in this hot summer. This is a climate change adapted parkrun.

Cassiobury Park on the edge of the Chilterns is the largest green space in Watford (77 hectares or 190 acres) established in 1909. It's a vast park with tree-lined avenues (oak, horse chestnut and lime) providing a canopy for the mildly undulating tarmacked paths. The start is a stampede uphill on a wide grassy area. Hearing the thunder of the charging runners on the baked ground reminded me of Bushy Park, just with fewer folk.

We had a hard working and successful run director in Glyn Jagger. As a director there's a marked maturity to his more recent parkrun releases. He combines the eye for detail of Hitchcock and Kubrick with the flair of Spielberg to ensure the smooth running of the event. Glyn's crew are equally as important. No run director can function without the necessary support of time lords, pre-event set up, course checker, funnel manager, finish tokens, post-event close down and token-sorting. If any part of the machine breaks down, then a parkrun is in jeopardy. We had 47 volunteers, one of the highest totals I've seen and indicative of an inclusive parkrun.

For the anniversary of parkrun restart, Watford Joggers kindly provided pacers. Realistically, after COVID-19 had taken its toll along with persistent knee problems, I soon lost the 28 min pacer (Hannah Jean McQuarrie) and it wasn't long before I was caught by the 30 min pacer, Adrian Heywood, accompanied by a convivial poodle. Having been almost pipped to the funnel in an uphill 'sprint' by a Labrador in Scotland earlier in the year, it was lovely to be escorted to another sub-30 parkrun by a four-legged friend. The 23 min pacer Navreet Singh landed bang on the time with their run as did the 28 min pacer Hannah. Top work all round by the Watford Joggers who deserve a huge thank you, I'm sure the high number of PBs reflects their efforts. Adrian and the poodle with no name (I should've asked!) certainly helped me maintain the pace needed to get into the funnel under 30 mins. It's been a hard year of running post-restart, I'm at least 3 mins slower on average and any kind of sub-30 is now the main ambition every week. Having run 38 parkruns since July 2021, my fastest post-restart time is quicker by over 5 mins (28:54 at Street) than my slowest (34:12 at Royal Tunbridge Wells in Kent) but is nowhere near my pre-COVID overall PB (25:12 at Norwich). For me, pre-and post-COVID times are universes not to be compared. The new normal is just fine.

First finishers Zico Field (new PB 18:14, also earned Junior 10 vest) and Sasha Birkin (19:34) needed no pacing inspiration to record quick times. We had 414 finishers, an encouraging 40 first timers, and 53 PBs. Paul Dreggs ran his 100th parkrun and earned the sought-after black running vest while Sarah Roberts, Valerie Green and Malcom Redfearn completed their 50th runs for the scarlet vest, congratulations to all. Praveen Nair, Cheyenne Chong and Archie Hearne all joined the 25 Club, the latter celebrating with a new PB (27:36). There's certainly some parkrunning talent at Cassiobury parkrun, long may it continue.

Tim's Tourist Tip-off

If you have a few hours to spend in the area post-parkrun, you should be exploring this wonderful park. As advised, I went for a wander after drinks and snacks. The Owl Tree with its green man carvings is worth a look as it's near to the bandstand. The fenced off Cedar of Lebanon will also catch your eye if you walk from the start area downhill. Following the parkland downhill will also take you to the meandering River Gade, the Grand Union Canal and the ancient Whippendell Wood. There's lots of grassland left uncut for pollinators such as bumblebees and other invertebrates. I noted numerous singing Roesel's bush-crickets and found many long-winged coneheads (also bush-crickets) in long grass by the River Gade.

Poetry Corner

The pacing poodle inspired a short haiku-like poem to celebrate Cassiobury, easily one of my favourite park parkruns:

sorry, poodle

in this sprint

one of us ain't trying

lost in a moment*

bandstand laughter

*This line is a song title by Watford's Sad Lovers and Giants. The last two lines were inspired by a wonderful chat with two parkrunners at The Cha Café. One said "I guess we'll never see you again" which made me think of the loneliness of parkrun tourism. I've met so many wonderful people on my journeys throughout the UK, but I've only known them for an hour or two at best. When the 100 different parkrun courses have been run by year end, I'm easing up on the touring and repeating some parkruns including in time, Cassiobury. There's the bonus of a mediocre course PB to strive for as well!

The bandstand at Cassiobury

36. ALNESS

Run Report: North by north-east, 06/08/2022

Motivated by the desire to run in most parts of the UK, I needed to spread the parkrun tourist net a little and explore some Scottish parkruns. In summer 2021 I ran Ganavan Sands with my son Joseph, while this year Edinburgh and Wallaceneuk in the Scottish Borders have been ticked off the list. But we needed to go further north. Our 2022 summer holiday was pleasantly interrupted by a stop at Glamis Castle in Angus. Sadly, despite the many tales of monsters in bricked up rooms, the only secret chamber we could find was inhabited by a Henry Hoover! Legendary Scottish poet Walter Scott's proclamation after an overnight stay in 1790 that he considered himself "too far from the living and somewhat too near to the dead" rang hollow. We absolutely loved Glamis though, but ultimately, we considered ourselves too near to an overpriced sausage roll, so we hit the road north.

Once in Inverness, we hiked up Ben Wyvis via An Cabar, both of which can be seen from the Yankee Pier of Alness parkrun. The Munro wasn't ideal preparation for a parkrun, but it's such a long way to travel from Essex that we had to make the most of it despite the hailstorm on the summit ridge which hit with full force, perhaps hinting at the mountain's alternative name 'The Hill of Terror!'

With spirits high and legs tired, we arrived at Alness on parkrun-eve for the obligatory course recce. I was excited about the varied course and chance to run beside Cromarty Firth on the Yankee Pier while my son was assessing PB potential. The views from the Pier are spectacular, the Firth complete with oil rigs and an abundance of marine wildlife. Dolphins, porpoises and whales can be seen if you're lucky. The return trip from the Pier provides a vista of Cnoc Fyrish (summit 453 m) with its cloud-slicing summit arches. The grassy habitats along the Yankee Pier and on the disused airfield are home to the moss carder bee, which we spotted on a purple knapweed flower, its ginger/yellow coat identifying this scarce species of flower-rich grasslands. The bee was also found near the summit of An Cabar earlier in the week and we saw it in 2021 near to Ganavan Sands parkrun! Scarce and declining bumblebees love Scottish parkruns.

On the morning of the run 58 athletes assembled in light rain, expertly looked after by 22 volunteers including the famous 'cone' (Tom Mathieson was the conehead today) who was dancing on the end of the Yankee Pier to the music of Billy Idol! The Pier is also longer than it seems. Do not be thrown by the cone! The feeling that you're near the colourful turnaround point is just an illusion. And don't be surprised when the cone turns up at the finish funnel before half of the parkrunners. There is a secret route for the cycling cone, steeped in folklore like the monster of Glamis…

We had pacers this week (21, 25, 28, 30 and 35 mins). A strategy of follow the one in front and hold off the one behind was adopted by Joseph and me to avoid 'termination' of our horological hopes as the pacers draw level in the last kilometre! Joseph's terminator was Robert Tomlin (25 min), mine was Al Bryce (30 min). My son Joseph ran in sunglasses to keep the rain off to record an overall parkrun PB of 23:30, successfully evading the 25 min pacer by trying to follow the 21 min pacer! I tried the technique further back but started to lose the 28 min pacer by the cone guy (that's Pier pressure!) and was dancing by myself (Billy Idol reference) across the deserted airfield! Luckily, there was enough energy in the defective tank to ward off Al and break 30 min. I was wary of the slight uphill incline to the finish on what is an otherwise pretty flat parkrun with minor undulations and differing terrain (mud, grass, concrete and tarmac) which make it a little harder than it may seem at first glance. There were also 7 PBs, this pacer lark has its merits. Congratulations to all athletes.

Alan Ross ran his 100th parkrun with a badge, congratulations to him for earning the coveted black running vest. Garry Dunbar completed his 50th parkrun for the red milestone running vest, the mark of a serious parkrunner. First finishers were the super quick Adam MacLellan (18:28) and Vikki Thompson (21:15). I must mention a strong effort from Laurence Rudkin (29:16, VM70-74) and the Alness Exocet Kaeden Thomas who overtook many of us after starting 3 min late to finish in 16th (23:20).

All of the Scottish parkruns I've run are picturesque from the sweeping sea views of Edinburgh and Ganavan Sands to the border hills of Wallaceneuk. Alness adds mountain views and has the distinctive Yankee Pier run and is of course, Home to the Cone as coined in David Bentley's grumpy guide to being the mythical marshal. Alness has yet to attract the significant student following it deserves. It should be on any parkrun tourist's wish list, student or otherwise.

Tim's Tourist Tip-off

If your legs can handle it after the parkrun, walk up through woodland to Cnoc Fyrish summit where there are stunning views of the Firth. On the summit is the Fyrish Monument, an 18th century folly which is composed of three central arches and four towers. It was erected in 1783 by local laird Sir Hector Munro. The folly was built during the Highland Clearances by starving local workers in return for famine relief. And if you like the look of wee Ben Wyvis, knock yourself out but leave at least one recovery day before the parkrun!

Poetry Corner

Dalmore Pier, also known as the Yankee Pier, was supposedly constructed by the US Navy in 1917-19 as part of the Submarine Mining base at nearby Dalmore Distillery. In the 1930s the area was used as a training ground for flying boats. It is also exposed to the elements as we found out. I include a short haiku poem from Scottish poet Claire Thom (first three lines published in The Japan Society's Haiku Corner, 2021) that sums up parkrun weather and my two lines in response (rain shadows):

> taking shelter
> under nature's umbrella –
> there's not much room
>
> in rain shadows
> where is there to hide

Claire grew up in Edinburgh and is a widely published poet who has lived in Cadiz for many years, working as an English teacher and examiner. A book of her haiku poems (Ever Forward) with watercolour illustrations by her dad, Colin Thom, was published in 2021.

Alness, home of the cone! Pictured with my son, Joseph

37. CROSBY

Run Report: You'll never walk, run, jog or jeff alone, 20/08/2022

For a visit to Liverpool with my son Joseph, our parkrun destination had to be Crosby on the Sefton coast. The windswept dunes and beach, dotted with Antony Gormley's Iron Men statues (Another Place), offers a stunning coastal location. The views of Welsh mountains (Carneddau range on a clear day) reminded us of Conwy parkrun (highly recommended) where those heights are much closer to home. Given the musical history of Liverpool, this run report will be delivered with a musical twist. Of course, the Beatles are first and foremost in Liverpool's musical legacy. They began as John Lennon's skiffle group, The Quarrymen, playing at the Cavern Club in the late 1950s. I can imagine a running style known as the Skiffle, particular to runners bending into a stiff Mersey breeze while shuffling through piles of sand on the prom. Assembled this morning were volunteer and parkrunning members of the skiffle ensemble, The Crosby Coasters:

Lead vocals – Emma O'Hanlon

A stunning performance on the microphone by Emma. As a junior Run Director (surely one of the youngest ever!) she not only conveyed the important run information but cracked some top jokes and had fun with the tourists who came from Essex, Sussex, Wigan and even Wolverhampton. I foresee a bright future for Emma as an RD.

Backing vocals – the liver birds

The mythical liver bird was probably a cormorant. It's a species often seen at Crosby in flight or spreading its wings to dry them. The dunes between the prom and grassy path to the finish funnel also have an abundance of the prickly sea holly. Look before you sit down!

Washboard – Bing's six pack

In the absence of a washboard marshal, Bing's six-pack is an adequate replacement, the wind gently strumming abs under a hi vis jacket. The crash helmet is pure Mersey punk. The skiffling run from the start to Bing is one of the most enjoyable experiences you can have running or walking at a parkrun. Runners' shadows on the sand are an ephemeral pleasure. A fleeting moment in time. I'd imagine it's hard to run the same parkrun twice at Crosby with the changing weather and seasons.

Clacker – half-way marshal

There was a wooden football clacker being rigorously spun at the half-way point by a jovial marshal, a reminder of Liverpool's football legacy.

Cigar box fiddle – timekeepers

This morning 147 athletes skiffled along the course and were accurately timed by David Todd and John O'Hanlon with their tiny cigar box recording thingies! There were 12 new personal bests, congratulations to all.

Washtub bass – first finishers

The bass is an essential part of the rhythm section of a skiffle band. The fast-paced rhythm of the run was maintained by first finishers Chris Jones (18:12) and Emma Andrew (25:13).

Comb and paper kazoo – milestones

Let's have a kazoo solo for all milestone makers. Michael Cochrane completed his 50th run and earned the sought-after scarlet running vest. Nigel Harvey joined the 25 Club to be eligible for the first milestone running vest. We also welcomed 7 newcomers to the skiffle mosh-pit that is parkrun. Let's hope they turn up next week!

Tim's Tourist Tip-off

As it was our first time in Liverpool, we had to visit the Cavern Club where the Beatles played hundreds of gigs in their early days. It's not the original venue opened in 1957 as a jazz club but it retains an intimate atmosphere with plenty of memorabilia for those interested in the history of rock and roll and the Merseybeat scene. Take time to have a pint, listen to the live music and be in awe of the bands that have played here. My favourites were the giant poster from The Who and Steven Van Zandt's guitar (he plays in Bruce Springsteen's E Street Band).

Poetry Corner

I include a short haiku poem from local poet runner Maria Isakova Bennett (first 3 lines) that sums up how parkrun brings people together and my 2 lines in response:

> I'm drawn
> by interlocking pieces
> balance
> between statues
> morning's shadow

Maria lives in Liverpool and is a widely published and prize-winning poet. Her latest poetry collection, Painting the Mersey in 17 Canvases (ISBN: 978173976091), was published by Hazel Press in March 2022 and is available from the London Review Bookshop. Go check it out! Maria is well known to local parkrunners having run an impressive 177 parkruns at Crosby.

One of Anthony Gormley's iron men

38. WICKFORD MEMORIAL

Run Report: The naked run! 27/08/2022

When I said to a friend that I was running Wickford Memorial parkrun they informed me that Britain's first naturist colony was founded in 1924 near Downham. For those of you that like costume dramas the Wickford nudist colony was even name-dropped in Downton Abbey! The folk of the Wickford nudist encampment mostly commuted, we assume fully clothed, into London giving the site the name Colony for City Men. Ideas of free love, closeness to nature and vegetarianism were promoted although the Wickford nudist camp only lasted two years as the ideas failed to catch on.

I'm not suggesting a nudist parkrun for the sake of public decency but the idea of closeness to nature is one that is certainly in evidence at Wickford Memorial parkrun with the run route passing along the River Crouch, through an area of woodland and by hedgerows. The meandering two and a bit lap route also has plenty of shade which in this summer of heatwaves makes it more tolerable for running and walking. Like Cassiobury parkrun in Watford which I ran a few weeks ago on a hot morning, Wickford Memorial parkrun is already climate change adapted. In future, people may flock to shady parkruns when it gets unbearably hot at locations without any cover at all. Apparently, the route does get muddy in winter though under the trees and in the grass section.

Wickford Memorial Park was established in 1949 to remember those men who died in World War II (WWII). The surprising slope (13 ft. or just over 4 m of elevation) of Wickimanjaro, climbed thrice, takes parkrunners up onto the summit plateau and the Avenue of Remembrance. The trees along the Avenue have plaques to remember those who died. There is also a Home Front Garden which was planted by the Wickford Memorial Association. It's certainly a picturesque and interesting location for a parkrun. I was pleasantly surprised at the attractive and varied tree-lined run route. It's well worth a tourist visit with the chance of a quick time too, as although Wickimanjaro saps your energy the third time it's not far from the finish funnel once you've summited. In short, it's not like the precipitous Catterhorn in Norfolk (Catton parkrun, Norwich)!!

Without further irrelevance, onto the run report. We had 156 athletes assembled for Event 61 supported by 24 fabulous volunteers who brought doughnuts, assorted cakes and several bananas. It's a friendly team of local people typical of parkruns up and down the UK. After a jocular run briefing by Nigel Williamson, we were off promptly. Going full frontal running-wise were first finishers Christopher King (18:52) and Southend AC's Sarah Jeffery (20:44). It was Sarah's 11th time as first finisher out of 13 runs at Wickford, an impressive achievement.

We had tourists from remote places such as Colchester, Southend and Dunstable. My own journey from Manningtree was a mere 42 miles. As a parkrun tourist at my 89th different global parkrun location (130th parkrun overall), the lay in was appreciated. I've run in most parts of the UK except the extreme (geographically speaking!) south-west, Lake District and Northern Ireland. Those oversights will hopefully be corrected before I reach my 100th different parkrun location (the Cowell Club) at Christmas.

Chatting to a runner afterwards, we discussed the physical problems of post-restart running and how we'd both lost around 3 minutes of time on average. We're both exponents of the 5K running technique known as the 'controlled fade' in which the first mile is around 40 secs ahead of your desired pace and you have time in the bank to be able to slowly drop (not literally) into the funnel ahead of time. It's worked for me in my last 8 parkruns where I've dipped under 30 mins by around 30 secs. If I start out slower, I still fade badly post-restart, so may as well go out hard and hang on (also known as the positive split)!

Milestones included James Shrimpton and Euan Ayers-Rist, both completing their 25th parkrun to earn the first official parkrun running vest. Geraldine Gapes completed her 100th volunteering stint while Keith Truscott brought up his 50th. Congratulations to all milestone achievers, especially Geraldine and Keith who help to ensure the parkrun runs smoothly.

Tim's Tourist Tip-off

Around 20 years ago I ran a butterfly and grasshopper identification walk at nearby Wick Country Park. The site is 50 acres of former agricultural land with around 2 km of trails which take you around ponds, along hedgerows and past WWII pillboxes. Well worth a post-parkrun walk or cool down run. Work on a 26 acre extension to Wickford Memorial Park has begun this year with an adjacent playing field being combined with the site. The improvements include planting of community orchards, wildflower meadows and trees. There will of course be paths to allow people to enjoy this new area along the River Crouch.

Poetry Corner

I finish with a couple of short haiku-like poems to capture the essence of Wickford Memorial parkrun:

leaving
heatwaves behind
riparian shade

no-one escapes
the shimmering incline

Running at Wickford © Wickford Memorial parkrun

39. MILDENHALL HUB

Run Report: Set the controls to the heart of the run!
30/09/2022

> Then at last, the mighty ship
> Descending on a point of flame
> Made contact with the human race at Mildenhall
>
> Let there be more light, Pink Floyd (1969)

There are many titles this run report could have had. My police record meant I considered 'walking on the moon' as the route passes the police station before traversing chalky moon rocks on the field section. There was also a serious draw towards 'larking around' given the proximity of the trail portion to the River Lark. And then there's the Mildenhall Treasure, a collection of Roman artefacts including plates and bowls from the 4th Century AD, discovered in 1942. Milden-haul or Milden-hoard were close contenders for title selection. Pink Floyd wrote of Mildenhall on a track (let there be more light) from their 1969 album 'A Saucerful of Secrets.' Pink Floyd imagined Mildenhall to be the first point of contact between aliens and humanity. In the end, despite my punk sensibilities, another Pink Floyd song 'set the controls to the heart of the sun' from A Saucerful of Secrets was corrupted to provide a lengthy report title for my visit to Mildenhall Hub.

Mildenhall Hub is not as you'd imagine, a giant broadband router, but a combined community and leisure facility. You can go for a swim before or after parkrun or read a book from the library which is next to the café. The Hub is a modern multipurpose building which makes it the perfect venue for Mildenhall Hub parkrun. Tourists have everything they need after a long drive. The course is two and a bit laps starting near the Hub building, incorporating tarmac and trail sections. The main heart of the laps is the off-road trail section which takes you past a dried-up pond, before switching to the ascent of Milimanjaro. The climb up the treacherous face to the chalky plateau peak is the slowest part of the parkrun which could get muddy in the winter. The path is also quite narrow and there's only room for two parkrunners abreast so good running etiquette is needed here. You pass by the actual chalk summit of Milimanjaro on your left before turning onto rough field edge paths which lead back to the tarmac and a lovely music playing marshal! I heard Coldplay at one point but never fear, it didn't put me off! I'll request Napalm Death on my return.

Mildenhall Hub parkrun commenced on 25th June at the start of the summer, today was Event 11. We had 97 athletes this morning supported by 15 essential volunteers. Run director Steve Davies delivered a witty run briefing with a colourful map of the course. We had tourists from Bedford, Essex, Oxford and Surrey. There was one official milestone as Tony Robinson ran his 50th parkrun to earn the striking scarlet vest. Also of note was Hayley Austin's 200th parkrun which, although not an official milestone, is mightily impressive and worthy of celebration. Congratulations to all. It was my 90th different global parkrun location as a tourist. The Cowell Club is so close now (100 different parkruns) I can taste it. For the record, 40 athletes beat the poet (me) over the hallowed 3.1 miles. A chasing mob armed with brooms or snooker cues could be one way of speeding me up in an alternative beat the poet segment of parkrun!!

First finishers were the supersonic Mark Hayward (16:52, new PB for Mildenhall) and Angela Joiner-Handy (20:50). Also noteworthy was Natasha Michael who'd just come off a nursing night shift to run 23:11. I need to thank Ryan Sheldrick (29:29) who ran with a buggy and kept me motivated throughout the parkrun. It really helped having someone to run with, particularly when the pace started to dip in the second half as the clouds parted and raised the temperature a few degrees. Despite the heat Jenny Osbourn (VW70-74) ran strongly to finish in 47:33.

After a lengthy chat with parkrun devotees in the café/library, which apparently is a weekly feature and not just me on one of my usual post-parkrun talkathons, I went for a wander around the trail portion of the course to see what insects and wildflowers were in the grassland. I heard Roesel's bush-crickets singing while field grasshoppers chirped from the chalky wasteland. There were also plenty of bees and butterflies out, many taking nectar from the purple greater knapweed flowers.

Tim's Tourist Tip-off

Just a few short miles up the A11 is Thetford Forest. I decided to go for a walk at Santon Downham, a place I loved growing up which has heathland habitat populated by scores of birds, insects and rare plants. After that I had planned a swim in the Little Ouse at St. Helen's Picnic Site but the water level wasn't much above my knees due to the drought! It was at least a cool-down after parkrun, if not a swim. Next time I'm taking a dip in the Mildenhall Hub pool.

Poetry Corner

I finish with a couple of short haiku-like poems to capture the essence of Mildenhall Hub:

>drought
>they tell me
>there's a river

>no point running
>dragonfly is faster

The only time I looked slightly athletic! © Mildenhall parkrun

40. RODING VALLEY

Run Report: Silent running, 10/09/2022

The sad news of Queen Elizabeth II's passing leant a contemplative atmosphere to Roding Valley parkrun. Many runners and walkers were present in black clothing to pay their respects to the Queen. There was a minute's silence before the parkrun began to honour the memory of our longest serving monarch (70 years). In 2017 an oak tree was planted during the Queen's Jubilee celebrations on the recreation ground, so the parkrun has a direct link to the monarchy. Roding Valley parkrun is sandwiched between the River Roding and the high ground of Epping Forest, a former royal hunting forest (more on that later).

The parkrun is a two-lap perambulation of Roding Valley Recreation Ground, mainly on grass. This morning, the grass had a covering of dew and was greener than during the summer's drought. Along the Roding there is a narrow-surfaced path, which I found helped maintain a little of the early pace on lap 1. The course has many meanders, notably taking athletes over Loughton Brook on a non-rickety wooden bridge! The bridge is a single file affair so good running etiquette is needed to ensure smooth passage for parkrunners. The route then loops around another grassy field before passing through a gap between a hedgerow and wooded area, snaking back to the start/finish area. I'd imagine the grassy parts of the course get very muddy in winter making the parkrun slower than one entirely on tarmac. To confirm this, Roding Valley was ranked 512th fastest parkrun out of the 706 UK events in an Athletics Weekly article on course difficulties and times.

This morning we had 130 parkrunners complete the course, aided by 15 top-notch volunteers. I particularly liked the marshal who called me Mr. Blow on the second lap, presumably referring to me puffing like a steam train! First finishers were Nathaniel Barre (18:50) and Zoe Oldfield (20:17), while we had one of the fastest tail-walkers I've seen in Amanda Overy (38:21) from Loughton AC. A new breed of tail-jeffer (jeffing is running and walking) is born.

After flogging a tired body around another parkrun course (my 91st different global one), only a sprint finish got me to another sub-30 time. It was a Mexican stand-off style sprint with places changing hands several times, no-one wanting to concede any ground. Len Edwards (29:46, VM75-79) came from nowhere to pip several of us into the finish funnel with one of the quickest sprints I've witnessed in the peloton. He's one to look over your shoulder for! The smiling assassin Mollie Heath (29:49) kept several of us at bay to record a new PB. Mollie was one of 79 others to beat the poet (29:52) including my son Joseph (25:09) and Beth Jones (24:31), an Orion Harrier who regularly tweets about running, amongst other things, on Twitter (@bethplodsalong).

The sole milestone was Nicola Guest's 25th parkrun for which she earns the first running vest. After the run, several people told me how hard they are finding parkrun post-restart. It seems that COVID has taken its toll on some folk who are struggling to regain anything like their former pace. I guess we just keep on turning up and giving it our best shot.

Tim's Tourist Tip-off

Away from the River Roding, itself a haven for wildlife, there is much to see in the Epping Forest area. Epping Forest was granted status as a royal hunting forest in the 12th century by Henry II. This meant that only royalty had the right to hunt deer in the Forest. Epping Forest is 2400 hectares (5900 acres) of ancient woodland (wooded since 1600 or before) and other habitats such as bog, heath and grassland. The royal connections are apparent at Queen Elizabeth's Hunting Lodge, a timber-framed building commissioned by Henry VIII. It was renovated for Elizabeth I in 1589.

Places like High Beach and the Epping Forest Visitor Centre are well worth a visit. High Beach affords a fine view over the Lee Valley. From here, you can also visit the secluded Forest plains with their bogs and heath. Sunshine Plain is one open area that has populations of insects which are scarce in Essex such as the common green grasshopper, which despite its name is anything but numerous in the county!

Poetry Corner

I end with a couple of short haiku-like poems to capture the essence of Roding Valley parkrun and the sad passing of the Queen:

pipped
to the finish
autumn sun

end of an era
yet, green grass

Queen Elizabeth's Hunting Lodge in Epping Forest

Victoria Dock with cable cars above

41. VICTORIA DOCK

Run Report: (Runnin' On) The Dock of the Bay, 17/09/2022

For my 92nd different global parkrun location, I travelled from Manningtree in north Essex on a sunny morning with a gentle yet cool breeze. Having left late, I was in a rush and accidentally parked in the Novotel carpark thinking it was a public multistorey. Such are the perils of tourism! The mistake only cost me £6 for an hour's parking. There are 20 minute short stay parking bays near the start but realistically you'd have to be running 14-15 mins to use those so not that helpful for us mere mortals! Public transport is best for this one.

Southwark parkrun was cancelled this morning due to the queue to see the Queen lying-in-state, so we had an influx of parkrunners from there. At the start, cable cars whirred by overhead. Leon Kong hopped onto a block to deliver the run briefing asking us to keep to the left, particularly through the wiggly bit near the ExCel Centre. He also cautioned against running up the steps near the start, the only appreciable elevation on the fastest course in the UK! The steps are a shortcut and there are other opportunities to cut corners on this course. Despite my school nickname of Corner Cutter Gardiner, I was able to avoid temptation this time! Runners and walkers also needed to avoid dropping in the drink, which all did. Joking aside there have been incidents in the past!

The parkrun is a two 'lap' out and back course, run entirely on flat, hard surfaces making it well suited for fast times. Sensing a 'quick' time post-restart, I ran like a lame Diplodocus fleeing from a T-Rex to record my fastest first mile for over two years (8:41). The course route took us past the steps of Mount Victoria (well, it's the course summit!), under the decorative cranes and through the ExCel Centre wiggly bit avoiding oncoming runners on the switch back storming along like Velociraptors late for breakfast. There is a Jurassic World Exhibition inside the ExCel at the moment which proclaims it'll be the closest you'll ever come to living dinosaurs. Given that my Tardis is out of action due to a faulty particle accelerator, they're not wrong! After the turnaround on both laps, the athletes are afforded a fine view of Canary Wharf skyscrapers.

This morning we had 178 parkrunners complete the course, aided by 10 Victorian volunteers. First finishers were the dockland express trains Oliver Neely (17:16) and Dee O'Brien (19:53). Tourists came from far and wide. I chatted to Robin and Benjamin Delaney from Tonbridge before the start, both as keen on the free cable car ride obtained using their barcodes (before 11am) than the run itself. During the run, I was overtaken by visually impaired runner and tourist Chris Blackabee with his guide. After the run, I talked with Ian Walwyn and Samantha McClory from the Black Pear Joggers club in Worcester.

Paul Game and Matthew Long both ran their 100th parkrun to earn the stunning black running vest. It was Zac Game's 10th parkrun earning him the Junior 10 running vest. Congratulations to all three.

Tim's Tourist Tip-off

As I needed to remove my vehicle forthwith from the Novotel carpark, I was unable to take advantage of the free cable car ride. However, it did mean I could relocate to London City Airport Travelodge (cheap parking) and explore the Thames Barrier Park on the north bank of the river. I work for the Environment Agency and it's our most important flood asset. I estimate that at least 8 parkrun courses are protected from tidal and freshwater flooding by the Thames Barrier along with 1.25 million people and £200 billion worth of property. The Thames-straddling structure is certainly an impressive feat of engineering. While in the park, I saw a cat being wheeled along in a pram and on leaving came across what appeared to be an East End punk tour with the guide wearing a Cockney Rejects' t-shirt.

Poetry Corner

I was reminded by a friend that it was International Batman Day. The Comic Con has also been held at the Excel Centre. To celebrate these facts, I end with a couple of short haiku-like poems:

> joker
> the watch
> wasn't kidding

> two faces
> to every run

42. SOUTHWARK

Run Report: Joy, we win! 01/10/2022

Dragged from slumber by a half six alarm, I set off for Southwark parkrun from north Essex for my 93rd different global location (134th parkrun). I ran Victoria Dock a couple of weeks ago, so it was time to go southside for a parkrun. The train strikes meant that driving or some manual form of self-propulsion were the only choices for transit which may have reduced numbers a little on the pre-marathon run. Southwark parkrun includes a section of the original 1981 London Marathon course down which a pace car drove! No such joy these days but a direct connection with the magnificent marathon's origins. The course was decorated with marathon-themed signs, a lovely touch that many enjoyed. My personal favourite was the Big Ben (yes, yes, I know it's just the bell name!) sign for 25 miles!

Marathon running originates from the first ultra-athlete Pheidippides (try saying that after a few drinks!) who ran 150 miles from Athens to Sparta in roughly two days in 490 AD. As a long-distance messenger his job was to ask the Spartans if they could help the Athenians fight the Persians in the Battle of Marathon. Unfortunately, the Spartans were busy/not ready, so he ran the 150 miles back to Athens in two days to relay this message. By then, the Athenians were already beating the Persians who were defeated without the Spartans. After this, Pheidippides then allegedly ran 25 miles from Marathon to Athens to relay the news that the Persians had been beaten. Reaching Athens, the exhausted Pheidippides exclaimed "Joy, we win" before collapsing and dying. It's a clear sign that too much running can be bad for you! It's also how I feel stumbling into the finish funnel these days…

It wasn't just marathon weekend that we celebrated, it was the 18th anniversary weekend of the start of parkrun in October 2004 by Paul Sinton-Hewitt. And finally, the morning also marked the launch of parkwalk, an initiative throughout October to encourage more walkers to take part. We certainly had plenty of walkers enjoying it this morning among the 421 athletes. Paul Williams completed his 103rd parkrun on crutches embodying the spirit of parkwalk. Let's not forget that dear old Pheidippides (assuming he slept 6 hours twice) was travelling at an average pace of around 14 minutes per mile (just over 4 miles per hour), a decent power-walk. He wasn't worried about times, just covering that incredible distance.

First finishers were Mintu Sidhu (17:22) and Eve Graham (19:54) racing around the fairly flat course with a few twists and turns and the odd gentle undulation. I really enjoyed it; the park is a green lung in the centre of London not far from Canary Wharf. I noticed a heron perched by the lake and numerous hawker dragonflies flitting around garden bushes before the off. Again, I became involved with a sprint finish battle which helped me squeak under my target time of 30 mins once more.

We had fabulous volunteers in abundance, 30 in total! Without them nothing would happen, we should be extremely thankful. You'll not meet a friendlier bunch in the parkrun universe. And don't forget to have a chat afterwards in the café, the selection of fried foods looked amazing.

Lauren Haslam joined the 100 Club and earned the black running vest. There were two new 25 Club entrants: Oliver Cooper and Emily Ingleton. Congratulations to them all. I was so pleased to run again with Tony Wilson who I ran with over 3 years long ago at Futakotamagawa parkrun in Tokyo while he was on holiday and I was at a haiku poetry conference. Sadly, neither of us had a view of Mount Fuji from the parkrun start that morning due to clouds hugging the volcanic cone. This is why I love parkrun. Forget the running, it's the people you meet.

Tim's Tourist Tip-off

After a long chat in the café with volunteers, I fancied a short trip to Greenwich Park for a snooze on the Royal Observatory slopes. Before a rest, I met some people putting up 'Please Don't Pee' signs for the marathon start and a team of Sprocker Spaniel sniffer dogs at the Pavilion Café. It's one of my favourite London parks for relaxing and I was able to get some kip on a scrap of acid grassland overlooking the city. A parkrun is body shattering these days when coupled with the early start required for tourism. I had the pleasure of a long queue through the Blackwall Tunnel on my way back to Manningtree. Can't have it all, I guess.

Poetry Corner

Driving between Southwark Park and Greenwich, I noticed some graffiti with a philosophical slant ("clouds never stay"). To celebrate this, I end with a short haiku-like poem which rearranges the words of the street art:

>
never
>
>stay
>
>clouds
>
>while
>
>we wait
>
>heron

London Marathon themed fun at Southwark

43. BURGESS

Run Report: Runopoly, 22/10/2022

"I never felt so much alike" – London Calling, The Clash

My third London parkrun in a row (94th different global parkrun location) after Victoria Dock and Southwark involved another early start. As a tourist from north Essex, I was particularly drawn to Burgess parkrun by its one lap course in Burgess Park, a green lung in inner London with views of the Shard (tallest building in UK at 309 m). One thing I'm learning from my London parkrun tour as I near the hallowed Cowell (run at 100 different parkrun locations) is the importance of green spaces in the capital for bringing communities together. Burgess Park has a lake on which swans and Egyptian geese can be seen from the bridge which intersects it. By the lake you also pass the Silent Raid memorial to the last Zeppelin bombing of London in 1917. There are numerous listed buildings that you pass on the run including Burgess Park Lime Kiln (built 1816) and St. George's Church (1824). There's also a mural of the famous but rarely seen Camberwell Beauty butterfly. The migrant butterfly is so named because two individuals were seen in nearby Camberwell in 1748. This is one to interest parkrun lepidopterist, John Buchanan, for his net is bigger than mine!

The course is a one lap affair mostly on tarmac with gentle undulations, most notably the underpass slope which feels like Ben Burgess on the homeward stretch. For perspective, the height of the Shard is the distance between the underpass and Bridge to Nowhere. You have to run 16 times the height of the Shard to complete a parkrun, how easy does that sound!!! Given that Old Kent Road lies at one end of the park, the run report HAS to be in Monopoly board game format from now on!

Go

With our worn-out boots (well, it's my go to Monopoly piece!) in the start area, run director Hannah Mumby delivered a lively briefing mentioning Victoria Popplett who will soon be migrating to Australia and dashing around parkruns there.

Community chest

The Ugandan crew regularly help with the running of the event, the familiar call of "Asante" (thank you in Swahili) can be heard from parkrunners to marshals. Burgess has been adopted by many Ugandan runners and volunteers, not necessarily from the local area. One runner comes from Slough every week while another (Sam) travels from Bow. Two weeks ago there was a colourful parkrun celebration of the 60th anniversary of Ugandan independence from the UK (9th October 1962). Long may the inclusivity of Burgess parkrun continue in these uncertain times. We need it more than ever.

Income tax

Parkrun is free to all, the only taxing thing is the running! It was less taxing for our super-quick first finishers, Dominic Blossom (17:09) and Alexa Parker (17:38).

Chance

As chance would have it, there were 65 PBs. Congratulations to all.

Just visiting

Looking at the results, we had parkrun tourists from distant places: Jacob Smith (East Chesire Harriers & Tameside Harriers AC) and Kevin Nicholson (Basingstoke & Mid Hants AC).

Electric company

October is parkwalk month, a very bright idea (groan, stay with me!) to encourage more people to participate in 5K walking. This morning we had the blue 'parkwalker' high vis marshal and Chris Vernon with the sticks putting in a sterling effort for the walkers. I have a fully overalled and masked speed walking alter ego Mike 'The Shape' Myers (PB: 39:12) who is resurrected most Halloweens! There are few things more satisfying than slowly reeling in and passing a parkrunner, remaining silent in keeping with the horror film character.

Free parking

Plenty of it around Addington Square. For more sustainable travel use the Tube.

Water works

It's been emotional. Robert Perry reached the Spartan milestone (300 parkruns) which although not official is special because it's a lot of committed running. If you don't know why it's called the Spartan milestone, google '300 film' and get working on that six-pack! Daniel Bangs and Gareth Jones completed their 25th parkruns and have earned the first milestone running vest, congratulations to them.

Go to jail

I got to step inside the garage-style lock-up for the parkrun equipment generously provided by Fowlds Café. I half expected a volunteer to say "Did you bring the money?" This morning free cakes and savouries were kindly laid on by the Clubhouse Café. Please support the café, they've done a wonderful job of supplying meals to local children during the cost-of-living crisis.

Super tax

You meet some interesting characters at parkrun who make things harder for themselves. Ben Salem passed into the funnel carrying a dumbbell in each hand. He runs a marathon distance (or more) most Saturdays carrying the dumbbells. Incredibly, today was his 91st marathon.

Do not pass go!

Remember to hand finish tokens back. Otherwise, go to parkrun jail.

Tim's Tourist Tip-off

If the weather is clement, why not stay in the park and explore for many of the reasons already mentioned. I'd also recommend a post-parkrun drink and bite to eat in Louie Louie café in Walworth, a short walk into town from Burgess Park. If you like listening to reggae or ska then this is the venue for you (and me!). Imagine a dub reggae DJ set from the great Don Letts. They also have a discount for parkrunners 10-11 am on Saturdays.

Poetry Corner

To celebrate a fantastic morning in Burgess Park, I end with three haiku-like poems:

crows

just once

scatter the spaniels

morning has meaning

a bridge to nowhere

when running

isn't hard enough

try dumbbells

Under the bridge at Burgess

44. HARROGATE

Run Report: Withnick and I, 29/10/2022

"Rejuvenate? I'm in a park and I'm practically dead" – Withnail

My attention was drawn to The Stray recently when Richard E. Grant shared a video of himself running around it on social media. As far as we know the Withnail and I actor has not yet taken part in Harrogate parkrun. With my interest in the parkrun raised by Withnail's pacy perambulation of The Stray, I travelled up for a long weekend with my son Joseph and good friend Nick.

The Stray is 200 acres (81 hectares) of public parkland in a long strip of grassland which joins the spa town's springs and wells together. In 1778, The Stray was set aside for public usage and unenclosed to protect it from illegal encroachments. In World War II trenches were dug on The Stray to prevent it being used as an airstrip by German planes. The Stray's Tewit Well with its familiar domed roof is named after the Tewit bird which is known elsewhere as the Peewit or Lapwing. Tewits still flock on The Stray to this day. The Stray is also part of a recent rewilding scheme to increase pollinator numbers by planting wildflowers and mowing areas less frequently. There's a mind-blowing estimate of 6-7 million crocuses (croci!) planted in the ancient grassland over the years.

The course is a straightforward 3 lap circuit of part of The Stray with half on grass and the other half on a tarmac path. It's a pleasant run for autumn with the leaves turning or in the spring when the crocuses are flowering. However, it can be muddy after heavy rain as we discovered. A pre-parkrun inspection on the Friday afternoon as we passed through revealed the grassy off-road sections to be fairly wet. We'd advise trail shoes if it's wet. We also met Michael Edwards, a fellow parkrun tourist also checking out the course beforehand.

On the morning, despite increasingly persistent rain we had 264 parkrunners for the Halloween event assisted more than ably by 20 vibrant volunteers. Tourists came from as far away as Margate with a group of Halloween costumed parkwalkers including Sharon Coughlan and Lulu Caps. The walkers were taking part in the October parkwalk initiative. We also had a tourist from Northern Ireland, Mark Ruck, completing his first non-Carrickfergus parkrun! Welcome to the tourist club, Mark. Be warned, it's an addiction that's hard to shake off!

Avoiding the puddle of eternal justice at the top of the incline and opening the stride on the tarmac were first finishers Gavin Lau (18:17) and Jenna McGrevey (19:26). There was only one milestone this week. Henry Waddington joined the Junior 10 club with a rapid 23:52. A total of 172 athletes beat the poet (30:30) as I faded like an old sock in a washing machine. Congratulations to Layla Stott (JW10: 30:10) and Yvonne Alys Skelton (30:26, 73% age grade) for trouncing me in the sprint. My son Joseph (27:53) and friend Nick also had good runs.

It became clear on the first lap that the off-road section past the toilet block had a gentle incline. I struggled with the mud, particularly on the 'ghost hill' section (elevation gained is around 28 ft., 8-9 m) past the toilets which I found tiring on the third lap. After the grassy sections though, the route to the start/finish area is all on tarmac and generally flat with a slight downhill gradient to offset the incline. This is where you can make up any time lost on the softer off-road portion.

After the parkrun we headed back to the car, noticing the thinning canopy of ash, chestnut and lime along Slingsby Walk. We also stopped for a bacon bap at Audsley Butchers on St. Winifreds Avenue West, highly recommended.

Tim's Tourist Tip-off

Against our better judgement we decided to hike up Great Whernside (summit 704 m) which is around 30 miles to the west of Harrogate on the edge of the Yorkshire Dales. It's a beautiful walk from Kettlewell to the Providence Pot cave entrance before zig zagging up to the summit via Hag Dyke. Returning to the converted Methodist Chapel in Greenhow where we were staying, we learned that it was once the haunt of the minister Joseph Kipling, the great grandfather of Rudyard Kipling. The author visited the village and may well have been to the Chapel.

Poetry Corner

To celebrate a fantastic morning at The Stray, I end with a couple of haiku-like poems for the wet morning:

trick or treat

depends

on the weather

the patter of feet

on rain

The Strays – Nick, Joseph and me!

45. SOUTHEND

Run Report: Runpowder plot, 05/11/2022

"Vague uncomfortable feeling you get when sitting on a seat that is still warm from somebody else's bottom" – Shoeburyness, The Meaning of Liff – Douglas Adams & John Lloyd.

Running for me these days is more akin to the entry for Shoeburyness in The Meaning of Liff. It's a vague uncomfortable feeling from a still warm bus seat as I push a failing frame around another 5K on the tourist trail! I've found parkrunning particularly difficult since the post-COVID restart through a combination of physical (knee injury) and mental health (bipolar) issues. I've gotten used to running 3-4 minutes slower than I used to but as Southend regular and friend Marc Outten told me recently, at least I'm still doing it. Maybe one day I'll be quicker but at the end of the run, it doesn't really matter. I must learn to enjoy the buttock warm bus seat as my tour around the UK nears its end. This morning marked my 96th different global parkrun location. The 100th different parkrun location (Cowell Club) is looming into view before year end. As it's Guy Fawkes parkrun, appropriately at Gunners Park, the run report will follow a firework theme…

Sparklers

This morning we had a conspiracy of 16 enthusiastic parkrun volunteers gathered at Gunners Park, three more than plotted with Guy Fawkes. There'll be no need for volunteers to flee anywhere upon discovery except a café for well-earned drinks afterwards. Kudos to the foam hand marshal too!

Roman candles

Popping out of the candle like balls of fire, 237 parkrunners assembled including a few walkers, no doubt spurred on by October's parkwalk initiative. It was heartening to see a tourist from Germany (Damian Norton) showing the true international nature of parkrun.

Skyrockets

Today's parkrun missiles were the first finishers Oliver Randall (16:36) and Chloe Fotherby (21:00). I'm sure they felt like exploding into a globe-like display of light at the end of their super-quick runs.

Ground spinners

Parkrun rewards those who repeatedly turn up. Reaching 'official' t-shirt milestones (or landmarks) this morning were the following parkrunners: Jesse Panthagani and Jonathan Rowley (new 100 Club members) and Dara Wylie (new 25 Club member). Congratulations to all.

Fountains

There were 22 PBs this morning on what proved to be a quick run despite the wind and rain. Parkrunners who particularly impressed included Claire Kirkland who ran a fire-cracking 22:43 to record her quickest parkrun so far. It was lovely to see Nigel Hill (49:32) record a new PB jeffing (run/walk) with his son, George.

Catherine wheels

All parkrunners wheeled three times around Gunners Park. The view of the sea is best enjoyed from the top of the lofty Mount Shoeji on the promenade. The mammoth size of this summit was hinted at by Lorna Stevenson in the run report for event 458 as 2 maybe 3 metres elevation! There's also a smaller peak of around 1-2 m near the start/finish area. I'm calling this one the Shoegar Loaf!

Tim's Tourist Tip-off

There's little need to leave Gunners Park for history lovers. The long structure stretching out into the mudflats which can be seen from the promenade section of the parkrun is a 2 km long anti-submarine boom built between 1950 and 1953 as a Cold War defence measure. It soon became obsolete due to the increasing threat from nuclear bombs delivered by aircraft. You also can't fail to notice the World War II Quick Firing Battery (built 1898-1900), the large structure just before the grassy turnaround point. There's also the Experimental Casemate built in 1872-3 on your right on the promenade and the 9.2 Inch Gun Emplacement to the left.

Poetry Corner

Following last week's poems from my trip to Harrogate parkrun, here are two short haiku-like poems inspired by this morning's parkrun:

getting carried
away by time
rain clouds

sprint finish
good luck beating cirrus

World War II Firing Battery along the Southend route

46. DULWICH

Run Report: The A-Z of Dulwich parkrun, 19/11/2022

Phyllis Pearsall of East Dulwich was the first compiler of the London A-Z in 1906. Armed with this obscure information, I'm compiling the Dulwich parkrun A-Z to tell the story of this morning's event:

A: Athletes, 524 to be precise this morning. We're all athletes because we have an athlete number. I will discuss this no further!

B: Barcode. It appears 35 people forgot it and registered the dreaded Unknown.

C: Catford. By the end of the parkrun I resembled the Hunchback of Notre Catford. Tough times since the COVID restart!

D: Dulwich Park Runners (DPR). Thousands of 'em! Well, not quite, but it was great to see so many in their green-and-white running vests. Apparently, this morning's run was a 5K club championship event.

E: Event 492.

F: First finishers were the lightning quick Jack Millar (15:25) and Johanna Vickers (19:08).

G: Gravel track. Available for those who need a more forgiving surface for the parkrun right next to the tarmac. Be knee kind.

H: Hill. The Dulwich Divot (it's at least 6 ft. elevation) is negotiated three times. Although this is a fast and flat course, there is a subtle incline to keep you honest with a difference in course elevation of 10 metres rising from west to east which you must of course negotiate three times. You won't notice it much until lap three.

I: Incline. See Hill.

J: Jimi Hendrix. See Ring-necked Parakeet. Keep the faith, there is a very tenuous link to the great musician!

K: Kick-off. It's 9 am, same time every week. Friends still ask me what day parkrun is on and what time it starts. How hard is it to remember? Charlatans!

L: Laps. Three of them I tell you. It's a smooth circular course with a very wide tarmac path so overtaking is quite straightforward. Just watch out for euphoric spaniels off the lead, those floppy ears can be lethal!

M: Milestones. Catherine Forward completed her 100th parkrun to enter the sought-after club and earn the black running vest. Andy Page became a half-centurion with his 50th run to become eligible for the striking scarlet vest. Samuel Bayliss, Alexander C. E. Rutter and James Smith ran their 25th parkruns and joined the first milestone club. And last but by no means least, Sebastian Hawkins joined the Junior 10 club (top time of 23:24, too). Congratulations to all milestoners.

N: Newbie. This morning we had 18 parkrunners completely new to parkrun. This is just the start of a wonderful journey for them.

O: Olympian. Last week, Olympic athlete (Tokyo 2020) Revée Walcott-Nolan ran a new course record time (16:03).

P: Personal best. Well done to the 88 parkrunners who achieved their PB for Dulwich.

Q: *Quercus*. The thick-trunked Turkey Oak (*Quercus cerris*) near the finish is impressive in girth, height and spread. Apparently, there's also a Toilet Oak near the conveniences.

R: Ring-necked Parakeets. I saw one fly overhead near the finish funnel during the run and couldn't escape the squawking racket from the treetops on a post-parkrun stroll. Urban legend has it that the parrots (native to Asia and sub-Saharan Africa) were first released on Carnaby Street by Jimi Hendrix and that some escaped from the set of The African Queen (1951) filmed in West London. Irrespective of how the exotic birds managed to escape into the wild, the green-coloured parakeet has become well established across London in the last few decades.

S: Southwark Slam. Complete all four parkruns in the London Borough of Southwark: Burgess, Dulwich, Peckham Rye and Southwark. I just need Peckham Rye for the Slam.

T: The African Queen. In my opinion, Bogart should have won the Oscar for Casablanca, not this film. Otherwise, see Ring-necked Parakeets.

U: Unknown. The phantom parkrunners. Still part of the numbers though and hopefully getting a good workout. See Barcode.

V: Volunteers. We had 24 dedicated volunteers who deserve our sincere gratitude. Special mention for run director Rob Murphy who brought calm to proceedings at the start and finish.

W: Walkers. The tail-walkers were Graeme Raeburn and Soo Yau, the latter finishing an overall swift parkrun with 48:58. The parkwalker was Catherine Gardiner complete with canine companion and the coolest surname. It's rare to get more than one Gardiner at a parkrun!

X: Xylem. Transport tissue in plants. The park has plenty of plants, check out the American Garden with its Rhododendrons. Bet you thought I'd stumble here? Tricky letter if truth be told.

Y: Yeovil Town Road Running Club. Tourists from Somerset in evidence.

Z: Zero turns: There are no abrupt turns. Enjoy the three smoothly arcing laps.

Tim's Tourist Tip-off

It's worth having a stroll around the Victorian park opened in 1890. Have a drink and something to eat in the Dulwich Clock Café before wandering around. It's the kind of park where you come across something interesting around every corner as the bushes and trees are effective screens. The American Garden is the most peaceful part while the park lodges near the Old College and Rosebery Gates are chocolate-box pretty. For art fans, Dulwich Picture Gallery is just outside the park.

Poetry Corner

To celebrate the wonderful parkrun here are two short haiku-like poems inspired by it, the second a tribute to Dulwich Park Runners who are a friendly running club growing and developing the social aspects of running as well as the technical:

<blockquote>
silence, please
the parakeets
have something to say

if you don't see the oak
why would you see the acorn?
</blockquote>

Look and listen out for parakeets along the route!

47. UNIVERSITY PARKS

Run Report: The Fellowship of the Run, 03/12/2022

A run report by Gollum c/o the parkrun poet, Tim Gardiner. With apologies to J.R.R. Tolkien fans....there are Tolkien quotes to spot!

We wants it, we needs it. Master says parkrun has them. Yes! Yes! University Parks parkrun, Oxford, Middle-earth. My preciouss is there. One token to rule them all. Ringses are soooo yesterday.

Kind lady, Jennifer Brooker, leads us to Park. She has no tokens in pocketses. Jennifer points out Dragon School by the path. Smaug is sleeping. Not a parkflyer these days. Black arrow found its mark.

We pass through an iron gate and sees hobbitses! There's a fellowship of 356 parkrunners. Some running clubs have travelled far. Go Be Runners (Yorkshire), Bristol Massive and Welsh National Opera are here. Here to steal preciouss!!! They cheats us! Runners of Rohan, we needs you!

From the Misty Mountains, Frosty the Snowman (Andrew Sulley) has come. Balrogs we need. The morning is cold. The fellowship is strong; we have hobbitses from Bedworth, Brisbane (Australia), Bristol (Eastville parkrun), Chelmsford (Central Park parkrun), Durham, Guildford, Leighton Buzzard, Lyme Park (parkrun is Staircase of Cirith Ungol), Manchester (Stretford), Newbury, Woking and Yorkshire.

Many volunteers (33). Where is master? We find run director, Trevor Williams. Why does he talk in riddles? Dogs on short lead. Children under 11 within armses reach. No Balrogs, Ringwraiths or giant spiders. May they rue this day! Milestones: Rhys Jones (25th parkrun), Harriet Brinton, Victoria Darke and Simon Hodkin (150th parkruns) and Emma Newton (200th parkrun). Simon Hodkin ran at his 100th different parkrun location, a feat humans call Cowell Club. Well done to tourist Simon! He's been there and back again!

So it begins. We're off. Two lapses of the Park. There are Ents! Trees everywhere: ash, blue spruce, copper beech, hawthorn, larch, lime, yew and many more. We avoid them. Try to trips us!! They sneaks up on Harriet Brinton, she trips. Frosty helps her. Kind snowman.

By the River Cherwell, the Dead Marshes (New Marston Meadows). The Bridge of Khazad-dûm forks right. You shall not pass! Bridge is steep and narrow. Fly, you fools! Like the Army of the Dead.

I missed Tolkien's Memorial Bench (installed by Tolkien Society in 1992). Fun! More fun than couches! We hates couches! A sign says they hates couches, too. Running gently up an incline, we passes start. Lap two is not fun. We thinks gentle incline is Lonely Mountain to tire legses.

First finishers Gavin Dale (16:27) and Olivia Martin (17:42) almost lap us. A hobbit passes us, it's Hayden Neale-Bates (JM11-14, 28:37, overall parkrun PB!!!). Quick! Quick! Through Fangorn Forest, Treebeard's domain. One last time past Minas Tirith, a cricket pavilion with turretses. We sees crane towers in distance! The eye of Sauron blinks from both.

Sign says turn left onto shady path. Reminds us of Moria. We hates dark. Balrogs live in dark. One hundred metres to go! The sign! It lies! It lies! Two hobbits in a fury scuttle past. We holds off an orc pack. They're not stealing my preciouss.

At the end of the funnel we gets the token! Yes! Yes! Yes! My preciousss. We wait. Invisibility must come when precious scanses. It must!! We hates being seen. Noooooooooooooo! The token scanner takes it from us!

We loves parkrun though. No puddle gazing. We sees wheelchair athlete Tiri Hughes power into the funnel. We sees Len Voralia, VM80-85, 523 parkruns! The lord of the runs.

Finally, we Dial-an-Eagle! Within seconds we sees one flying. That's a red kite! Tricksy! The Great Eagles are on their way....

Poetry Corner

To celebrate this wonderful parkrun with connections to J.R.R. Tolkien who studied at Oxford University, here are two short haiku-like poems inspired by it all:

> leafless beech
> the run goes on
> and on and on

> cold morning
> where is the fire in my legs

Chasing a snowman at University Parks, Oxford

48. BELTON HOUSE

Run Report: It's the most wonderful time of the deer, 24/12/2022

'Twas the night before parkrun, when all thro' the cabin,
Not a gadget was stirring, not even a Garmin.

Clement Clarke Moore's classic poem 'Twas the night before Christmas' has appeared in more run reports over the years than you can shake a carrot at. The opening rhyming couplet serves parkrun well, but it's what follows that applies to Belton House parkrun:

With a little old driver, so lively and quick,
I knew in a moment it must be St. Nick.
More rapid than eagles his coursers they came,
And he whistled, and shouted, and call'd them by name:
"Now! Dasher, now! Dancer, now! Prancer, and Vixen,
"On! Comet, on! Cupid, on! Donner and Blitzen.

Reindeer are in the same family of animals (Cervidae) as the deer that on occasion can be seen at Belton House parkrun. Although Belton House obviously has no reindeer, it has an abundance of fallow deer which were absent this Christmas Eve. The extensive deer park through which the parkrun course runs is part of the 1300 acres of land surrounding Belton House which was built between 1685 and 1688 by Sir John Brownlow. The picturesque parkrun is a must visit for any Yellowbelly badge seekers (all runs completed in Lincolnshire). Yellowbelly is apparently a slang term for a person born in Lincolnshire. I've enjoyed two parkruns in the county so far: Lincoln and Market Rasen Racecourse. Belton House was supposed to be my Cowell (100 different global locations) but the snow and ice meant I had to stay local and not tour last weekend. I was joined by my son Joseph this morning and an old university friend, Nick Harpur, who filled the role of jolly St. Nick. My only concession to the festivities was a Santa hat (worn by my son in the end!) after an unfortunate incident where my Santa trousers fell down near the finish funnel in a previous parkrun. It was great to see so many parkrunners in fancy dress, the undoubted highlight for me were the wise men. One of them ran a 23 min parkrun in wellies, a Christmas miracle if ever we needed one.

The tale of the parkrun before Christmas is best told through the medium of Santa's reindeer:

Dasher – on this festive morning we had 15 PBs, notably Oscar Jones (16:19) and Niall Gilchrist (16:56)

Dancer – 336 parkrunners danced around the course in the absence of deer (or reindeer!)

Prancer – bounding around the course in inelegant style was the parkrun poet (me), being easily bested by 170 athletes including my son, Joseph. My friend St. Nick (Harpur) ran strongly before his evening duties squeezing down chimneys, beating me by a short head in an unexpectedly fast sprint finish. Of course, we know it's not a race….

Comet – like comets of dust and ice, tourists had travelled far to be part of the fun. We had athletes from Cambridge, Derby, Manningtree (Essex), Peterborough, Scunthorpe and Sleaford.

Cupid – we need to share the love with the 26 volunteers. Without them nothing would happen on Saturday mornings. Well, apart from more sleep that is.

Donner – the old Dutch name (Donder) of this reindeer means 'thunder.' Let's have thunderous applause for the milestones: Martin Carter and Daniel Sheard (100th parkruns), Mark Hill and Wayne Searle (50th parkruns), while Rachel Kay, Kevin Kettle, Rachel Podesta, Eleanor Reeve, Emily Spridgens and Cj Walker completed their 25th parkruns to join the first milestone club.

Blitzen – the old Dutch name of Blixem means 'lightning.' The lightning bolts finishing first were Sophia Tucker (20:37) and William Tucker (17:39)

Poetry Corner

To mark the festive parkrun here are two haiku poems to celebrate the open parkland of Belton House:

oh! deer
at least you're fast
when you want to be

late breakfast
I can't outrun Santa

49. NORTHALA FIELDS

Run Report: Ghost of parkrun presents, 25/12/2022

"The cold within him froze his old features, nipped his pointed nose, shrivelled his cheek, stiffened his gait; made his eyes red, his thin lips blue" Charles Dickens, A Christmas Carol.

"Bah! Humbug!" growled Scrooge. The unspecified budget hotel was not cheap enough. He'd also been told that a Christmas Day parkrun was the best medicine for a mean spirit. Fortunately the bed was comfortable, the shower hot and the vending machine well stocked with midnight treats. The early start for Northala Fields parkrun (event no. 375) was not something Scrooge was looking forward to. Nothing could spread joy to this novice runner's life. Absolutely nothing. He hadn't set an alarm and would probably oversleep.

Ghost of parkrun past

Scrooge had managed to get off to sleep after a last-minute adjustment of the room's storage heater temperature. The Do No Disturb sign was hanging on the door to dissuade cleaners from coming in early. Around one o' clock, a heavy clanking noise could be heard in the corridor outside. The door opened slowly. Backlit by corridor lighting was the ghost of Marley, Scrooge's old running buddy. Scrooge had given up exercising some time ago after Marley passed away. The fun had gone out of it. It's running after all.

Startled, Scrooge sat up in bed. "I have come to warn you about the dangers of not exercising, Scrooge" boomed Marley. "These chains around my body are heavy, yours will be heavier if you don't get fit again at parkruns!" "You don't even have to run, they have parkwalk now, plus there's a variety of stimulating volunteer roles" the ghost added. After this dire warning, Marley dematerialised leaving Scrooge in the dark.

Ghost of parkrun present

At two o' clock, the room was bathed in white light. Before the freshly awakened Scrooge stood a giant with a crown of holly. "Let me show you what you'll be missing if you have a lay in." With that he conjured up the parkrun story in a ball of glowing mist.

Scrooge could see the Christmas Day event unfold at Northala Fields. Beside the four grassy mounds, a mountain range constructed of the old Wembley Stadium waste rubble, 304 parkrunners assembled to complete the festive parkrun. Among the parkrunner pack were tourists from as far afield as Watford. Scrooge almost smiled as he saw the mass of jeffers, runners and walkers snake around the course, some in festive fancy dress. A hint of joy spread across his grizzled countenance as he counted 29 volunteers in all. "It's like a real community" he remarked to the ghost. "Yes, every week at nine o' clock it happens" the jolly giant responded.

Scrooge could see Tiny Tim, the parkrun poet, hauling his large frame along the paths spurred on by his unofficial pacer, Carmen To. "Tim's completed his 100th different global parkrun location at Northala Fields, entering the Cowell Club" whispered the ghost so as not to disturb those in adjacent rooms. Also present was Roderick Hoffman, timekeeping as a volunteer. He's run at 345 different events globally, a truly incredible achievement. Those who run their first 50 events at 50 different locations enter the Hoffman Club as he was the first to achieve the feat. Colin Harris, who's run 723 parkruns was running in his blue 500 milestone top. Official milestones were numerous. Stephen Plummer ran his 250th parkrun with a superb time of 19:25. Jose Gresa, Jacky Mercey and Jessica Wong all completed their 100th parkruns to earn the black running vest, while Phil Manly finished his 50th run to become eligible for the scarlet milestone top. And last but not least, the 25 milestones (purple vest): Anuj Sharma, Esher Jhooti and Samantha Wiggins. Well done to all parkrunners!

"And what of the first finishers?" croaked Scrooge. "Today, the supersonic superstars were Ben Waterman (16:01) and Francesca Boote (19:53)" replied the gentle ghost. Scrooge thought to himself that it all looked such fun. There were cakes aplenty and even Nepalese dumplings! "If you don't turn up to parkrun later, you will be missing out on all of this fun and associated health benefits" the ghost warned Scrooge before fading into the blackness of the room. Scrooge felt positive about the future. He was definitely going to run in six hours' time.

Ghost of parkrun yet to come

It was only an hour later that Scrooge was awakened by the last of the three ghosts. The ghost before him was dressed in a black robe and held a scythe. "To be honest, there's no need for me in this story" the deathly spectre opined. "But I'm here now, so let's look at your parkrunning future" he added, with a clacking sound from skeletal jaws.

Scrooge was treated to a wondrous visitation of parkrun touring, meeting new people and gaining the health benefits of regular exercise. Future Christmases would be affairs filled with laughter and probably cake/dumplings. The loneliness of Scrooge's life would be reduced somewhat. He would become a more charitable and generous man, perhaps even donating to his local parkrun. Plus, he'd give Tiny Tim the funding to continue his parkrun touring.

With that positivity the spectre departed the room, slipping like fog under the door. Scrooge checked his alarm was set and fell back to sleep. No more would he doubt parkrun.

Poetry Corner

To celebrate Scrooge's festive parkrun here are two haiku poems for Northala Fields at Christmas:

ghosts
the legs
of Christmas past

snail mound
luckily the trail is flat

50. FOUNTAINS ABBEY

Run Report: More kestrel manoeuvres in the park, 31/12/2022

Note: there is a connection between the legend of Robin Hood and Fountains Abbey…

Robin Hood was a jolly fellow. "If Joan of Arc had a heart…" he'd sing from his favourite song 'Maid of Orleans' by Orchestral Manoeuvres in the Dark (OMD). The video for the song featured Fountains Abbey, a ruined Cistercian monastery in Studley Royal Park. Robin was keen on the parkrun at Fountains Abbey, so quickened his pace towards the River Skell which skirts the scattered ruins as the gatekeeper prevents entry to the parkrun at nine (so don't be late!). The ruined walls and tower are the domain of ghostly choirs and the odd kestrel seeking a perch. Besides, the Green Man had told him to challenge Friar Tuck to a parkrun; the loser carries the winner over the river on his back. The great thing about being a legendary character is you never grow old (Robin is in VM640-645 age category) and at the parkrun start, Robin could see that Friar Tuck had feasted well at Fountains Abbey over the centuries. Robin imagined that he could easily beat Tuck on the (gently) undulating paths of the parkrun.

Including the merry pair there were 494 parkrunners gathered for the New Year's Eve event with light rain just before the start. A jovial band of 30 volunteers busily organised the proceedings so that all was ready to go on time. Robin felt like twanging an arrow into the air in a poetic show of defiance but was restrained by the reserved friar on health and safety grounds. This morning Gordon Wilson joined a small club of extremely dedicated parkrunners by running his 500th parkrun. Gordon has been parkrunning since 2011 with an impressive PB of 21:03. Running their 100th parkruns were Helene Greenwood and Sue Moul while Sally Williamson and Graham Turner joined the 50 Club. The newest milestone club (25 runs) was reached by Ben Sellars and Abigail Lewsey. Congratulations to all parkrunners.

Robin and Tuck had learned to be wary of tourists fearing they may be the Sheriff of Nottingham's men in disguise. There were visitors from Cambridge, Bradford, Leeds, London, Newcastle, Shropshire and Germany. Those from Nottingham were treated with the suspicion their presence deserved! The parkrun poet (Tim Gardiner) who had travelled up from Essex reached his 100th different UK parkrun location this morning (143 parkruns overall). He was heard saying that Fountains Abbey is easily one of the best parkruns, ranking it alongside events like Alness (Scotland), Cinder Track (Whitby), Conwy and Severn Bridge.

The parkrunners were off at nine, the large crowd snaking past the ruins. The parkrun is an undulating two lap perambulation of the Fountains Abbey grounds which could be considered Yorkshire flat (approx. 135 ft. of elevation gain). Robin noticed a kestrel hovering far above the first gentle incline, presumably keeping its eye out for a vole or mouse. Passing over the Rustic Bridge, Robin felt like challenging Tuck to a sword fight but resisted knocking him into the drink before ascending the first significant incline at the end of lap one which is a test of the running resolve. On the second lap, the narrow boardwalk across the Skell represented another chance to dunk Tuck into the water but this was admirably resisted. They passed the labouring parkrun poet by the impressive Half Moon Pond which was still as a millpond. By this time the first finishers Tom Calvert (16:57) and Helene Greenwood (18:38) had already burst into the finish funnel. They were quicker than even Alan-A-Dale in his pomp when he beat Guy of Gisborne and the Sheriff of Nottingham in the Belvoir Bubble Run. That happy thought made Robin smile for he was far away from the secluded glades of Sherwood Forest.

The finish funnel loomed into view for the rebellious pair after the Temple of Piety. Robin had gone out too fast as usual while Tuck's obvious lack of match fitness was apparent as the final incline to the funnel started to bite. Robin managed to sneak into the finish funnel ahead of the friar who had dined too well at Fountains Abbey through the mythical ages. Both were given a finish token by Pamela Vinicombe ably supported by Fiona Alder. Robin and Tuck thanked Pamela, Fiona and the funnel manager, Karen Tulley. They seemed to have an equitable method of token distribution. Robin had no need to stage an ambush to ensure that tokens could be distributed to those less fortunate. Besides, Robin Hood's Well was nearby. The Sherwood legend had returned to Fountains Abbey and had no desire to sully his reputation with an ill-advised heist.

Having lost to Robin, Tuck protested that the parkrun was not a race. However, to retain his honour Tuck was forced to wade through the Skell carrying the outlaw on his back. He cursed his bad luck and general lack of stamina over 5K. He must stay off the local ale. A kestrel landed on the tower and watched the comical river crossing. The parkrun was not only an idyllic place to jeff, run or walk but also a haven for wildlife. It reminded Robin of home.

Poetry Corner

Fountains Abbey was known to the English novelist and poet Letitia Elizabeth Landon (1802-1838). The opening stanza of her poem simply titled 'Fountains Abbey' is an evocative and gothic portrayal of the wonderful heritage site:

Never more, when the day is o'er,
Will the lonely vespers sound;
No bells are ringing—no monks are singing,
When the moonlight falls around.

Landon was widely admired for her writing by contemporaries including Edgar Allan Poe in the US and Tennyson in the UK. Landon was prone to melancholy which influenced her powerful words. Sadly, she died in mysterious circumstances of poisoning by prussic acid. The haiku-like poem which follows is dedicated to her memory:

old pond

half moon

half water

the breeze chants

its own song

One of the best

APPENDIX 1. THE EXTRA ONES

FUTAKOTAMAGAWA, JAPAN

Run Report: The journey itself is home! 14/09/2019

My third trip to Tokyo was to attend the World Haiku Association Conference. Haiku are short (usually 3 lines) Japanese poems inspired by nature. The event organised by eminent writer, Ban'ya Natsuishi, drew together poets from all over the world including Italy, Mongolia, Nepal, and the USA.

In this way, parkrun is much like haiku, bringing tourists from across the world to celebrate running in a friendly community. My first run in Japan was the 5 km circuit around the Imperial Palace, a quite majestic venue with hundreds of people running around it every day. In the evening, it's a near continuous parade of runners on the pavements, all looping around the beautiful Palace moats and walls. For anyone visiting Tokyo, the Imperial Palace circuit is a must; the largest unofficial parkrun in the world!

Arriving early at Futakotamagawa, I met many tourists from London and Australia by the flood defence alive with crickets and grasshoppers (including 7-8 cm long-headed locusts, see photo).

bank steps
thank god we run
on the flat path

The location of the park is beside the Tama River, which flows down through the hills near Fussa; along which many rare species of animal and plant can be found.

storm flow

who can outsprint

Tama River

A view of distant Fuji is afforded on a clear day, but the peak can be frustratingly elusive in the rainy autumn season as I discovered with clouds obscuring its majesty. The famous haiku poet of Edo Japan, Matsuo Bashō, eluded to that in one of my favourite haiku: how pleasant / just once not to see / Fuji through mist. The title of this run report is also a famous quote by Bashō.

the rumble

of a train above

floodplain stones

Today, we had 147 samurai run, jog or walk the route, supported by 22 magnificent volunteers. A total of 59 people beat the poet (time 26:53), who faded like the snows of Fuji-san in spring.

long grass

runners scatter

green locusts

The most wonderful sight greeted me at the finish funnel, a murmuration of birds, possibly starlings.

murmuration
the beat of my heart
in the funnel

blossom breeze
runners scatter across
the start line

the last snow
on Mount Fuji
parkrun blossoms

big in Japan
marshals discuss
the hilliest course

DALBY FOREST

Run Report: I am the walrus! 01/01/2023

The undead need stimulation. Dracula had grown bored over the centuries hanging around Whitby Abbey. The three sisters (often referred to as brides) had goaded him once too often and were banished to Dalby Forest on the North York Moors. Legend would have you believe that they were turned into sandstone pillars on high Staindale Moor by a vampire curse.

The parkrun poet didn't believe any of this gothic nonsense instead choosing Dalby Forest for a parkrun due to its natural setting on the North York Moors. Five species of bat is far more impressive than the vampire stories. He'd been meaning to run Dalby Forest for several years. Sadly, the poet's running seemed cursed since the parkrun restart after the relaxation of COVID rules. Running felt like trudging through treacle every week so the forest paths seemed preferable to pounding concrete and tarmac.

The New Year's Day parkrun attracted a spirited gathering of 173 athletes ably supported by 17 volunteers. Early excitement was provided by a fallen tree along the course which was quickly shifted by three volunteers. There was also talk of the walrus which had come ashore at nearby Scarborough even leading to the New Year fireworks being cancelled in the town to avoid disturbance. Apparently, it was the first sighting of a walrus in Yorkshire.

Among the marshalling hi-vis heroes was parkrun tourist and Dalby regular, Helen Patricia Rutter. She'd help spur the poet on and break the running curse! Milestones for the first parkrun of

2023 were Marion Bets running her 100th parkrun to earn the striking black running vest and Sally Brown and Shirley Field reaching the 50 Club. Congratulations to all milestone achievers. Aside from the parkrun poet from Essex there were tourists from Derby and even further-flung Milton Keynes.

The run began at nine as usual, the early skirmishes between parkrunners taking place on the higher paths of the course among the conifers. The one lap course winds its way around the forest taking in some gently undulating paths and loops before the main elevation on the run, a snaking path uphill. After the hillslope, parkrunners follow a path along the beck for the last mile meandering like the watercourse in the dale. This section has a slight incline which you may not necessarily notice in the legs while you're enjoying one of the finest views in the parkrun universe. There's also bridges to cross. You then face the Dalby coup de grâce; a zig zag uphill path to the finish funnel. It's shorter than the infamous Fountains Abbey finish incline but it's still Yorkshire flat!

The first finishers Luke Beresford (17:49) and Christine Dover (20:46) were probably done before the poet had reached the open dale. He felt his legs begin to regain some of their strength of old though! On the right side of the path in the trees, the poet caught sight of a strange looking marshal in a black cape. His legs were instantly struck with the kind of aching pain he'd known for some time before the gothic marshal disappeared and a bat flew into the trees. The cheering of a conventionally dressed marshal (hi-vis jacket) spurred him on to beat the affliction. Two more times this happened. A black-robed marshal hidden in the trees would materialise, intensifying the poet's calf pain, before vanishing. Luckily there were more enthusiastic marshals to spur the poet on to beat the apparent curse that was afflicting his legs, particularly those long-troublesome calf muscles. The fabulous marshals this morning were Helen and Andy Rutter, Sue

Thomason, Richard Newman and Stuart Gordon who turned out to effectively enthuse parkrunners with their energy. On this New Year morning 14 athletes recorded new personal bests. Notably, Ruth Friend (JW11-14) smashed her parkrun PB by over two minutes to run 21:08 (77.05% age grade).

The parkrun poet completed his 102nd different global parkrun location (101st UK parkrun and 7th location in Yorkshire) and mused on the identity of the three marshals dressed in black and how their appearance seemed to curse his legs! That the hi-vis heroes restored his energy is testament to the volunteer work that is put into parkrun.

Taking a stroll up to the Bridestones on Staindale Moor after the parkrun, the poet noticed something odd. Three of the Bridestones seemed to have distinct faces like sisters huddled together on the lonely hillside. As he approached one of the stones to climb it, he felt searing pain in his calf muscles….

Poetry Corner

The North York Moors is one of my favourite places to visit due to the rolling moorland and isolated hilltops. Roseberry Topping is a modest hill worth a climb. A circular walk taking in the Wainstones scramble is not one to miss either. In Dalby Forest there is much to enjoy including the Bridestones on Staindale Moor. Many famous writers have been inspired by the landscape of the North York Moors and the surroundings including Lewis Carroll (La Rosa Hotel, Whitby), Bram Stoker (Dracula in Whitby), William Wordsworth (married in Brompton) and Alf White (James Herriot). A good friend of mine and superb poet, Claire Everett, lives in nearby Northallerton. Claire writes excellent haiku such as this one (published in Sketchbook, October 2010) which could easily apply to Dalby Forest:

forest walk
scent of pine needles
threaded with rain

I am similarly inspired by forest walks and runs and respond to one of my favourite parkruns with this haiku-like poem:

the breeze's curse
tempered by birch
showing off
the stream can run
down the rabbit hole
on THAT final hill
Cheshire Cat grin

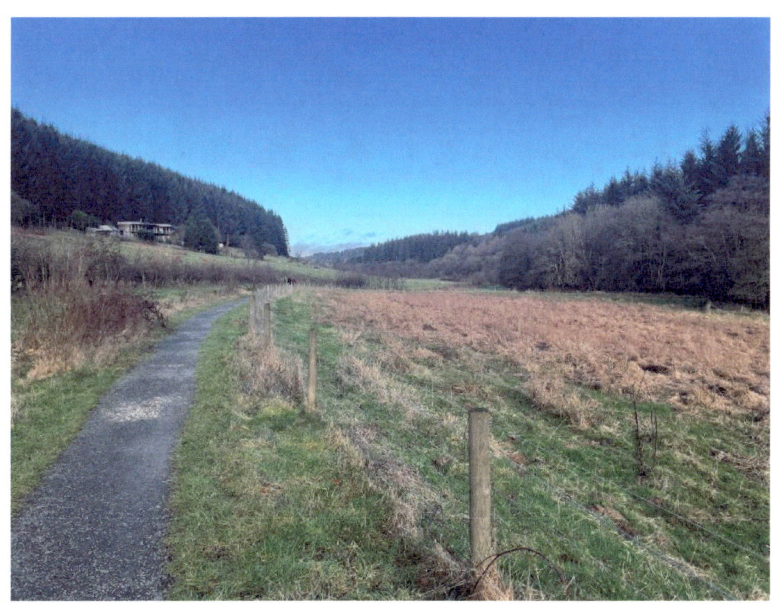

Final meadow run at Dalby Forest

Dalby Forest upwards flat section

TOWN MOOR

Event run 19/08/2023

A stay over in Newcastle on the way up to Scotland meant we got to run Town Moor. The park is larger than Central Park in New York at 400 hectares (1000 acres) and has fine views over Tyneside due to its elevated location. Freemen from the city are allowed to graze cattle on Town Moor and you may see cows beside the parkrun course. The Hoppings is held every year in the park and is said to be Europe's largest travelling funfair with over 300,000 visitors annually. Town Moor had a racecourse until 1881 when the last race was held. Remains of the earthworks can still be seen. Racing then focused primarily on Gosforth Park which is now Newcastle Racecourse. Gosforth Park was of course famously featured in the British gangster classic, Get Carter (1971), starring Michael Caine. Many shooting locations for the film including the High Level and Swing Bridges are distinctive features of Newcastle to this day. The Great North Run starts along the western edge of Town Moor making the park a hub for running.

My son Joseph ran the parkrun on 19/08/2023 while I speed walked under my alter ego Mike 'the shape' Myers. It's a fairly easy course to follow and I was joined in the walking by two parkrunners for a pleasant chat and stroll around the grassy meadows and tree lined paths. There were over 500 parkrunners and walkers on the day we took part making this one of the largest parkruns on the poetry tour outside of Bushy.

"You're a big man, but you're in bad shape. With me, it's a full-time job. Now behave yourself."

– Jack Carter (Michael Caine), Get Carter (1971).

AVIEMORE

Run Report: Thunder in the glutes, 24/08/2024

Motivated by the desire to run in most parts of the UK and 100 different events (Cowell Club), I needed to spread the parkrun tourist net a little and explore some Scottish parkruns to reach the Cowell Club target. In summer 2021, I ran Ganavan Sands with my son Joseph, while Alness, Edinburgh and Wallaceneuk (Scottish Borders) were ticked off the list in 2022 as I passed the 100 event mark. Injury curtailed running in 2023, but occasional speed walking is possible. Given the beautiful nature of Aviemore that turned out to be the best way for me to enjoy the course with its sweeping views of the Cairngorms in the open sections where the heather was a purple haze. Appropriately for the Highlands, the course is not flat but undulating with approximately 36 metres of elevation gain (c. 120 feet) and a significant downhill section after the turnaround on this oot and back course. My son, Joseph, found the hill just before the finish a shock to the system!

I'll tell the tale of this parkrun through the medium of motorcycle films or famous movie bike scenes due to the Thunder in the Glens motorbiking event in Aviemore which saw thousands of leather clad fun seekers descend on the town:

The Wild Run

Imagine Marlon Brando on a motorbike. Whaddya got?! Well, we had 117 finishers and 10 superb volunteers. Nothing happens without the volunteers, please consider rebelling against your running instincts and helping out from time to time. The music at the turnaround point was a nice touch from the marshal there. My tune on the turn back was Hotel California by the Eagles. You can check out anytime you like, but you can never leave! Sounds like an oot and back course and possibly the addiction that is parkrun!

The Great Escape

Riding the proverbial bike into the barbed wire after a long journey were tourists from South Africa, Essex and the south-west. No tourist was marooned in the metaphorical wire for long as they were shepherded to the course start by the fabulous volunteers after an amusing and informative run briefing.

Easy Runner

You got a helmet? Well good for you. The easy runners who sped along the course as if saddled on an invisible Harley Davidson were Billy Sutherland (17:16, JM11-14) and Sarah Hodgson (18:58); two incredible first finishing times.

Every which way but loose

There were 7 new PBs and a swell of first timers to Aviemore composed of a large number of tourists and maybe a few bikers from Thunder in the Glens. It was also lovely to see Andrew Aird once more, parkrun ambassador and runner from Dunfermline. I'd run with him before at Wallaceneuk parkrun a couple of years ago.

Terminator

They'll be back. Speeding off on their Harley Fat Boys into new parkrun clubs were Matthew Bennasar (100 parkruns), Martyn Grisdale (50 parkruns), Sarah Swinden (25 parkruns), Max Murray (JM10) and Elena Szender (JW10). Let's hope they can terminate further parkrun targets! Hasta la vista, parkrunners!

Mad Max

All fuel injected speed machines need to stop off and top up in the superb Route 7 Café. If you miss out, you will be as mad as Max Rockatansky on an open forest road!

Poetry Corner

On my longish parkwalk, I composed the following haiku poems for Aviemore parkrun, inspired by the beautiful surroundings:

rain shadow –
a dragonfly darts
out and back

mountain view –
even the walker
slows down

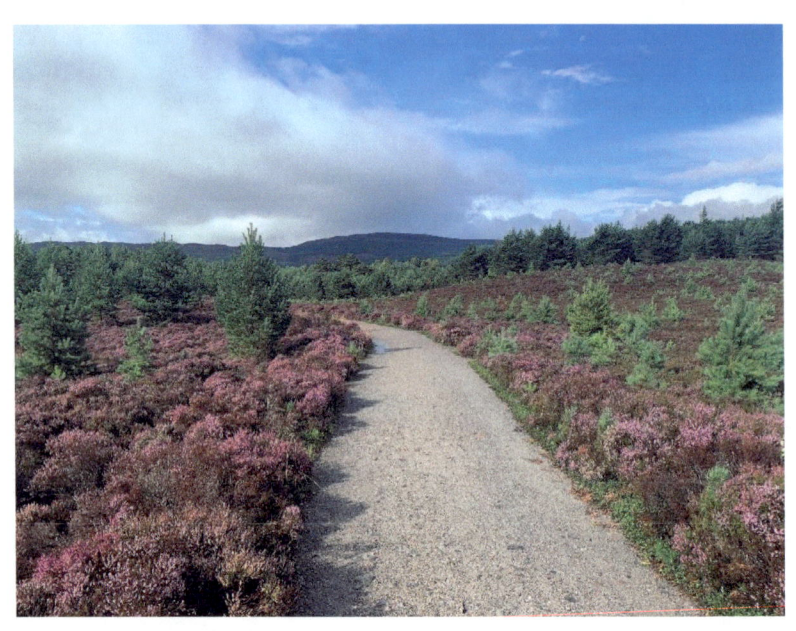

The open moorland views of Aviemore parkrun

WHINLATTER FOREST FREEDOM RUN

The hilliest parkrun in the UK (674 feet of elevation gain) was tackled in the summer of 2020 after COVID lockdown restrictions were relaxed and my son (Joseph) and I could travel up to the Lake District for a break. We were warned of its steepness so had been training on local 'hills' in Essex for a few weeks prior to our attempt. I was prepared for a fair amount of walking and some spectacular views to compensate. Arriving at the handily marked up start of the parkrun (remembering fixed signage is rare for most parkruns), we sprinted off downhill for the first few hundred metres thinking Whinlatter wasn't as hard as we'd been led to believe! We were blanketed in drizzly rain for most of the run so no chance of overheating. However, the track started to wind upwards on some steep slopes following the route as it makes its way up through dense forest. In open areas without tree cover there are breath-taking views, if there's any breath left to take!

Reaching the 'summit' of the run we tanked downhill, Joseph disappointed to know that we had to switch back and do more climbing before the downhill finish. When it did arrive, we took full advantage of the downward sloping track to the finish and the Gruffalo owl. Exhausted, we reflected on a slow parkrun time, but a fantastic course for its scenery and forest. Although not an 'official' parkrun for us, we would certainly rank it as one of the hardest we've run and that includes the not quicksand of the impossible Great Yarmouth North Beach. It is a favourite parkrun of hill-loving writer, Eileen Jones. Eileen includes a description of the event in her recent book 'p is for parkrun – a journal from A to Z'.

Whinlatter Forest, view from a flattish section

The Yankee Pier, Alness

DAD'S ARMY SCREENPLAY SERIES - THETFORD

EPISODE I. THEY DON'T LIKE IT UPHILL

"Early to bed, early to rise…." E.C. Cochran – quoted by Captain Mainwaring

Kate Measures asked me a long time ago if I could write a Dad's Army themed run report as the series was filmed in Thetford town centre and in other Breckland locations such as Santon Downham. Given that my running has been temporarily curtailed due to a flare up of an old knee injury, voluntourism is the order of the day. This morning, I was one of the Meadow Marshals as they're known. This grassy section of the course including a short slope is known as the Dreadow to some and the two laps can be very muddy in winter. But don't panic, here is the run report as a Dad's Army TV screenplay. I can hear the ghost of John Le Mesurier saying "Do you think that's wise, sir?"

Scene 1. Volunteer meet up

The sky is clear blue and it's warmer than of late. On the grass overlooking the Thetford Priory ruins, 23 volunteers assemble to look after the platoon of 184 parkrunners. Run director, Kelly McGill, is doing a fine job of making sure it all happens on time and in orderly fashion. There are tourists from Attleborough, Banham, Hastings, North Carolina, St. Albans, Washington State and Wisbech! There are also 20 first timers, including some from Thetford. There are members from 18 running clubs and Avani Solutions representing the charity Only A Pavement Away which helps homeless people, prison leavers and veterans find stable employment.

A mystery volunteer, let's call him Marshal Jones, is running late and noticeably out of breath after a sprint through the underpass as he starts chatting to Kelly and Kate.

Kelly: No need to rush, we still have ten minutes until the start.

Marshal Jones: Don't panic, DON'T PANIC!

Kate: Calm down. You're one of the Meadow Marshals at the top of the slope.

Marshal Jones: They don't like it uphill!

Kate: You stupid boy!

After more inane and frankly unnecessary banter from Marshal Jones he jogs off to his spot in the Dreadow with its notoriously uneven ground and propensity for waterlogging in winter.

Scene 2. The Meadow Marshals

Marshal Jones is at the top of the Thetford traverse. Parkrunners will pass this way twice before heading off to the finish. A few minutes elapse before the front runners appear. A train of athletes follows in their wake winding around the lumpy grassland. One parkrunner is playing hit records.

Marshal Jones: Permission to speak, sir?

The parkrunner nods.

Marshal Jones: I love these tunes, especially Under Pressure by Bowie and Queen. Have you got any Vera Lynn or failing that, Glenn Miller?

The parkrun poet is also marshalling in the Dreadow. He's known for writing dodgy run reports which pay scant attention to the affairs of the morning. Marshal Jones shouts across the grass to him.

Marshal Jones: Sir, I should like to volunteer to be the one to write the run report this week.

Parkrun poet: Oh do be quiet boy!

The parkrunners are generally a friendly bunch, though. A Norwich City fan runs past in a striking yellow and green Canary shirt.

Marshal Jones: Who's your favourite Norwich player?

Ebony Harker: Pukki!!

Marshal Jones: Mine too, reminds me of Harry Ware, a Norwich centre-forward who played in the War League!

The tailwalker Vasanti Patel and parkwalker Bernadette Bowden pass by twice making sure that all parkrunners are accounted for.

Scene 3. The finish

Marshal Jones follows the parkrunners back to the finish where he finds out that the first finishers were Matt Webster (18:49, new PB) and Sarah Palmer (22:54). There were 14 personal bests including Ellie Godfrey (clear Dad's Army surname!) and Ebony Harker.

Marshal Jones: I enjoyed that. I'm off to blow raspberries at the Captain Mainwaring statue in the town centre before visiting the Dad's Army Museum.

Kate: You stupid boy!

Thetford in the snow

EPISODE II: A PLATOON OF PACERS

Thetford parkrunner Kate Le Measurier asked me a long time ago if I could write a Dad's Army themed run report as the series was filmed in Thetford and in other Breckland locations such as Santon Downham. Given that my running has been temporarily curtailed due to a flare up of an old knee injury, voluntourism is the order of the day. This morning, I was a troll marshalling by the bridge making sure folk didn't take the wrong route. Here is the run report as Episode II of the Dad's Army TV screenplay (Episode I was for event 477, featuring Private Jones) featuring none other than Private Godfrey. Event 479 was quite the Dad's Army knees up in fact. We had Privates Danny, Katherine and Nicholas Jones, Private Martin Godfrey, Privates Karl, Kathryn and Tracy Walker and for good measure, Hannah Fox (aka Marcia Jones, née Fox).

Scene 1. The platoon

A cloudy sky slowly clears and it's warmer than of late. By the Priory ruins, 38 volunteers assemble to look after the large field of 214 parkrunners. This morning we have 14 pacers ranging from 22 to 42 minutes. Run director Robert Whittaker does a fine job of organising the troops that would please Captain Mainwaring. There are tourists from Bicester (Oxfordshire), Farnham (Surrey), London and Rayleigh (Essex) so we have a geographically widespread field! Marshal Jones has left the duties to his three namesakes. He's working in the butchers (J. Jones) in town. Jonesy often drives his van slowly around town with a string of sausages hanging out the back!

As usual Marshal Godfrey is late to arrive, but he always turns up in the end and his loyalty to the parkrun is unwavering. He often brings his sister's upside-down cakes for the volunteers. Run director Robert greets him by the table.

Robert: Good to see you Godfrey, glad you've made it.

Marshal Godfrey: I didn't want to disappoint you, sir.

Robert: Well done, Godfrey. Any relevant marshalling experience, I know you've not done this role before?

Marshal Godfrey: I was in the sports department of the Civil Service Stores for several years.

Robert: That'll do, you can marshal by the bridge with that parkrun poet fellow. Make sure no-one goes the wrong way and all parkrunners complete the two laps of the dreadow and river sections.

Marshal Godfrey: Will do. Thank you, sir.

Not wishing to be late Marshal Godfrey wanders slowly off to his spot by the bridge followed by an inquisitive dragonfly which keeps buzzing his high vis jacket.

Scene 2. Holding the bridge

By the bridge the marshals natter before the first runners appear making their way towards the bridge. The parkrun poet is wearing a Jog Division running vest, while the photographer Geoffrey Herschell has a Stiff Little Fingers (SLF) t-shirt with the slogan 'Everyone is Someone' which couldn't be more appropriate for parkrun.

Marshal Godfrey: I'm not familiar with these new-fangled bands.

Parkrun poet: Check out SLF, you might like punk. Think rock n' roll, but played quicker.

Marshal Godfrey: Oh dear, it might be a little loud for me.

Parkrun poet: We'll go to a gig in Norwich one day!

Marshal Godfrey: The second cup of tea was a mistake. Do you think I might be excused?

Parkrun poet: Quick into the bushes before the runners get here. I'll make sure they go the right way.

The first finishers, Owen Stocker (19:23) and Isla Winslow (21:25, new PB!), are not too familiar with the course so need guidance on the correct route and number of laps. Ten minutes pass and there's no sign of Marshall Godfrey appearing from the bushes. The poet investigates and finds him lying motionless on a patch of tall grass.

Parkrun poet: Marshal Godfrey, what the devil is up with you?

His eyes blink open like Smaug in the lonely mountain.

Marshal Godfrey: I must've dozed off!

The poet helps Godfrey to his feet and the pair regain their positions by the bridge, continuing to shepherd the parkrunners. Two 500 t-shirts pass by belonging to Nick J Haigh (505 parkruns) and Sue Round (547 parkruns). James Camilleri is running his 50th parkrun while Bobby Hutchinson joins the Junior 10 Club and can wear the white running vest with pride from now on.

Scene 3. The swing ball spill

As the last runners and tail walker pass by, the pair decide to pack up the post and tape which prevent parkrunners from taking a detour. Marshal Godfrey struggles to untie the tape around the bridge rails, cursing his luck. Eventually, he manages to do so and the parkrun poet picks up the swing ball base. Unbeknownst to him, he's supposed to pour the water out before picking it up. The water spills out during transit all down the parkrun poet's trousers! Godfrey can't resist a chuckle. This pair have taken bumbling to a new level.

Marshal Godfrey: Do you think I might be excused?

Leaving the weak bladdered Godfrey behind in the bushes, the parkrun poet returns to the start. Out of the platoon of pacers, only Hugh Worsnop hit the mark dead on with 33:00. Bragging rights are his until next month.

Fun at Thetford parkrun © Thetford parkrun

EPISODE III: DON'T TELL HIM, PIKE

Thetford parkrunner Kate Le Measurier asked me a long time ago if I could write a Dad's Army themed run report as the series was filmed in Thetford and in other Breckland locations such as Santon Downham. Given that my running has been temporarily curtailed due to a flare up of an old knee injury, voluntourism is the order of the day. This morning, I was in the sought-after marshalling location known as Dog Poo Corner. The bin was particularly exotic with a fully laden black bag with a distinctive whiff left on the ground next to it!

Here is the run report as Episode III of the Dad's Army TV screenplay featuring the youthfully exuberant Private Pike.

Scene 1. You stupid boy

It's a little cooler than when Private Godfrey marshalled. He's had a rough night on the sherry so is unable to make it to the Priory ruins on time where 23 volunteers assemble to look after 165 parkrunners. No pacers this week but there are tourists from Colchester, Hoddeston, Kent, Manningtree, Northampton and Peterborough. Unlike Godfrey, Private Pike is not delayed by a leaky bladder or nap after breakfast and reports for marshalling duties on time.

Parkrun poet: Good to see you, Private Pike, glad you've made it. Hope you're in a good mood, you're marshalling Dog Poo Corner with me!

Private Pike: Oh no, I'll tell mum.

Parkrun poet: You stupid boy……c'mon, let's get going. Don't want to be late to the marshalling spot by the dog bin.

Private Pike: Ooh, this walkie talkie is exciting, Captain Mainwaring would love it!

They wander off, Pike playing with the walkie talkie radio he'd been given by the run director. He'd be even more annoying if he worked out you had to hold the button down to talk!

Scene 2. By the bin

Private Pike moans about the smell from the dog bin. He also reminiscences about the time the platoon came across a German U-boat commander.

Private Pike: Do you get submarines this far up river, Mr. Poet?

Parkrun poet: You stupid boy…..

Private Pike: Oh goody, they've started! The runners are coming….

Parkrun poet: Yes, just act your usual over-excited self, you'll be perfect at this marshalling lark.

Private Pike: Captain Mainwaring will be so proud. You'll tell him about my marshalling, won't you?

Parkrun poet: Of course. Now, clap, cheer and encourage like you've never done before.

The unlikely pair of parkrun marshals see the runners and walkers pass by twice. This morning, we have the usual whippet, plus two lassies trotting past adding canine interest to the fray.

It's pleasing to see a decent crop of parkwalkers, too, enjoying the summer air and company. The first finishers, David Loomes (18:48) and Sarah Palmer (22:50), pass by on their way to super quick times for the course.

While high fiving a walker, Pike is nearly mown down by a bike careering along the path from the housing estate.

Parkrun poet: Be careful, Pike, let's not have any Dad's Army comedy capers this morning.

Private Pike: Whistle while you work, the cyclist was a twerp!

Thetford regular, Nick J Haigh, runs past in his 500 t-shirt, that's a lot of running. Martin Gooderham is running his 200th parkrun, an unofficial milestone, while three runners join the 25 Club: Harry Robinson, Michael Scott and Raymond Riddell. And last but by no means least, Isabelle Little joins the Junior 10 Club with an excellent time of 24:57. There were 8 PBs, congratulations to all the speedsters.

Scene 3. Don't tell him, Pike!

As the last runners and tail walker pass by, the pair decide to trudge back to the finish area. Pike moans that he'd love to have been out there running this morning, which is sharply rebutted by the parkrun poet who emphasises the need for volunteers to enable parkruns to run smoothly.

Private Pike: I'm off to check for submarines in the river.

Parkrun poet: You'll do no such thing, you stupid boy....

As the pair near the finish, a volunteer wanders over.

Parkrun volunteer: It's a hot day for military wear but the contrast between khaki and pink high vis really works for you. What is your name?

Parkrun poet: Don't tell him, Pike.

Parkrun volunteer: Pike! Your name will also go on the volunteer roster.

Pike has enjoyed volunteering. He's not been reprimanded by Captain Mainwaring for starters or mocked by Uncle Arthur. He'll be back.

Severn Bridge parkrun, one of the best

EPISODE IV: DO YOU THINK THAT'S WISE, SIR?

Thetford parkrunner Kate Le Measurier asked me a long time ago if I could write a Dad's Army themed run report as the series was filmed in Thetford and other Breckland locations such as Santon Downham. Given that my running has been temporarily curtailed due to a flare up of an old knee injury, voluntourism is the order of the day. This morning, I was barcode scanning at the finish. Here is the run report as Episode IV of the Dad's Army TV screenplay featuring none other than the gentle charm of Sergeant Arthur Wilson.

Scene 1. I think they've rumbled us…

Private Pike has harangued his Uncle Arthur (Sergeant Wilson) into barcode scanning at today's parkrun. He's volunteered just to shut Pike up. Sergeant Wilson will probably thrive in the genteel atmosphere of the post-parkrun barcode scanning arena. He's part of a large platoon of 35 volunteers assembled to look after 170 parkrunners. The volunteer ranks are bolstered by pacers due to it being the first parkrun of the month. There's a good spread of pacers from 21 to 50 mins. Tourists have come from as far away as Harlow, Hornchurch, King's Lynn, Markshall, Rendlesham Forest, Sittingbourne and Westmill. Sergeant Wilson says that Rendlesham Forest is just like Santon Downham and equally as beautiful with its pines and heathland. Rendlesham Forest has a parkrun too, one of the best in East Anglia according to the parkrun poet who has just turned up still half asleep after a drive from Manningtree in Essex.

Parkrun poet: Good morning, Sergeant Wilson. You should bring the platoon along for next month's pacer week….

Sergeant Wilson: Do you think that's wise, sir?

Parkrun poet: Private Godfrey could easily pace 25 mins.

Sergeant Wilson: Do you think that's wise, sir?

Parkrun poet: Alright, 90 mins might be more appropriate.

Sergeant Wilson: The dear fellow needs frequent stops owing to a weak bladder.

As Kate Le Measurier finishes an excellent run briefing involving a brief mention of nurses' uniforms (8th July is parkrun for the NHS), the runners and walkers are off.

Scene 2. Would you scan, sir?

Sergeant Wilson seems confused by the iPhone and parkrun volunteer app cursing everything from Captain Mainwaring's pomposity to a dodgy Walmington banger he bought from J. Jones in town.

Parkrun poet: You got that blasted contraption under control yet, sir?

Sergeant Wilson: I think so, just in time for the first finishers, old bean.

Parkrun poet: You'll soon be beeping away without a care.

Sergeant Wilson: Let's hope so, sir.

Parkrun poet: Here we go, good luck Sergeant.

The unlikely barcode buddies happily scan the runners and walkers after they exit the funnel. There's the odd curse or two from Wilson as an array of wrist bands, print outs and QR codes are presented for scanning.

The first finishers, Harry Robinson (19:10, new PB and first sub-20) and Eloise R Stradling (21:33) have run quick times for the course.

Gary Malliband is running his 200th parkrun, an unofficial milestone, while two runners join the 100 Club: Simon Hill and Richard Snow. There were 19 PBs, congratulations to all the speedsters.

Scene 3. I can see that, sir!

As the last parkrunners are scanned, thoughts turn to the final platoon member to volunteer in a couple of weeks.

Sergeant Wilson: You know, I think Captain Mainwaring would love parkrun.

Parkrun poet: He's born to lead, sir.

Sergeant Wilson: Well, don't tell him that when he turns up. Run directing may not be for him, likes the sound of his own voice too much. Besides, Kate Le Measurier does a jolly good job.

Parkrun poet: I reckon he'd bungle timekeeping and probably drop the finish tokens so it probably rules out those roles, too. We'd be doooooommmmmmed!

Sergeant Wilson: I can see that, sir! Most unreliable.

Parkrun poet: To be honest, funnel manager sounds official enough.

Sergeant Wilson: Indeed, it does. I'll make sure I mention it to him at the bank on Monday.

Parkrun poet: And don't forget to tell young Pike how much you enjoyed barcode scanning. He does love to hear how his Uncle Arthur is getting on.

Sergeant Wilson: Well you see, I've known his mother for a number of years….

My son in the mud at Royal Tunbridge Wells

Spring morning at Street with a view of Glastonbury Tor

APPENDIX 2. TOURISTS WHO'VE MATCHED WITH THE 100 PARKRUN LOCATIONS IN GLADE RUNNER (2020) AND SILENT RUNNING (2024)

Nigel Cronin	84
Simon Berry	80
Michael Ball	71
Gary Parr	69
Stephen Richard Dawson	66
John Buchanan	61
Ian Richardson	61
David Milton	60
Sean Dunn	58
Steve Langley	55
Mark Shotton	51
Nigel Harris	50
Susan Cartwright	47
Andrew Harvey	47
Phil Olson	43
John Biggins	42
Carri Vendy	39
Derek Hood	38
Kristina Bright	37
Nicola Forwood	36
Robin Defoe	33
Heather Houghton	33
Alice Noyes	33
Terry Hubbard	30
Francesca Palmer	30
Richard Smith	30
Sarah Mackay	28
George Pake	28
Robert Clark	27
Paul Wain	27
Bradley Day	26
Phil Walker	25
Comme Letia	24
Richard Robinson	21
Mark Watlow	21
Carly Watson	21
Richard Furze	20
Tracey Salisbury	20

Jayne Turner	20
Steve Streeting	19
Jenni Spafford	18
Adele Bovington	17
Anthony O'Brien	17
Lisa Wright	17
Glen Clive	16
Simon Grigor	16
Eileen Jones	16
Richard Leaper	16
Janet Todd	16
Paul Brown	15
JJ Colby	15
Rich Harrison	15
Robert William	15
Clearbrook	14
Mike Harper	14
Dawn Hill Hughson	14
Peter Johnson	14
Andrew Pick	14
Dave Playforth	14
Carol Baker	13
Louise Caroline	13
Carol Cooke	13
Chris Lee	13
Natasha Michael	13
Melanie Miller	13
Martin Palmieri	13
Jenny Ball	12
Alan Byron	12
Jenny Dimmick	12
Aileen Galvin	12
Colin Hare	12
Paul Jeffrey	12
James Lester	12
Paul Wakeford	12
Bob Jones	11
Sue May	11
Lou Mayer	11
John Route	11
Roy Warden	11
Dave Johnson	10
Lucy Salmon	10

Richard Sun	10
Callie Vee	10
Russell Barnes-Heath	9
Rob Biggs	9
Jeff Chandler	9
Paul Dudbridge	9
Brad Ehlen	9
Emma Lougheed	9
Trevor Meadowcroft	9
Patricia Morris	9
Janice Parker	9
Emma Powell	9
Jason Newell	9
Tony Reeves	9
Neil Tiley	9
Cheryl Booker	8
Paul Hawgood	8
Heide Swift	8
Mark Swindells	8
Ian Walwyn	8
Becks Brooks	7
Joanne Campbell	7
Sacha Fox	7
Rachael Hodgson	7
Graham Holland	7
Olly Hughes	7
Brioni Izzard	7
Karen Larkin	7
Kate Stanton	7
John Taylor	7
Jo Vince	7
Alan Blagburn	6
Joanna Burden	6
Thierry Chew	6
Andy Coward	6
Michelle Craker	6
David Harpin	6
Emma Louise	6
Holly Ochiltree	6
Mark Parsons	6
Ruth Perkins	6
Michael Stanley	6
Paul Aird	5

Louise Bastock	5
Neil Bayliss	5
Tammy Cook	5
Peter Coombs	5
David Draycott	5
Sue Freegard	5
Ollie Frogg	5
Jeff Hardy	5
KBee	5
John MacInnes	5
Roger Pangbourne	5
Jack Revely	5
Philip Richardson	5
Elizabeth Sheridan	5
Matt Sprack	5
Alex Wilson	5
Laura Baker	4
Sally Bowden	4
Fiona Boyce	4
Andy Brook	4
Ken Coggin	4
Karen Connal	4
Robert Duncan	4
Tony Hardy	4
Helen Harrell	4
Deb Jenks	4
Lorraine Longmuir	4
Christie Nisbet	4
Michael O'Donoghue	4
Julie Osgerby	4
Andy Wilkinson	4
Mark Williamson	4
Jaroslaw Zajac	4
Felicity Crotty	3
Joan Gibson	3
Zoe Griffiths	3
James Harrison	3
Ian Hook	3
Seren James	3
Jane Mac	3
Ann Susan Officer	3
David Taylor	3
Sarah Tregear	3

Mike Warriner	3
David Chambers	2
Jason V. Clift-Jones	2
Harry Graeme Goddard	2
Lee Halliday	2
David James	2
Roz Mogg	2
Nadege Rutter	2
Miriam Salo	2
Charlotte Widdows	2
Rachel Fryer	1
Tim Gallagher	1
Neil Patience	1
Darren J Pead	1
Tim White	1

Tourists selected from a request on UK parkrun tourists facebook group on 11 Feb 2023 and subsequent updates.

Shorne Woods parkrun

THE 100 POETRY PARKRUNS

Alness	Great Cornard	Peel
Alton Water	Great Dunmow	Pegwell Bay
Belton House	Great Notley	Rendlesham Forest
Billericay	Great Yarmouth	Roding Valley
Blickling	Hackney Marshes	Royal Tunbridge Wells
Brandon CP	Harrogate	Rutland Water
Brockenhurst	Harwich	Sandringham
Brundall	Harleston Magpies	Severn Bridge
Burgess	Haverhill	Sewerby
Bury St. Edmunds	Highwoods	Sheringham
Bushy	Humber Bridge	Shorne Woods
Cassiobury	Hunstanton	Shrewsbury
Castle Park	Ipswich	Sizewell
Catton	Kesgrave	Sloughbottom
Chalkwell Beach	King's Lynn	Soham Village College
Chelmsford Central	Lincoln	Southend
Chilton Fields	Lingwood	Southwark
Clacton Seafront	Littleport	South Woodham Fer.
Clare Castle	Loch Neaton	Storeys Field
Clumber Park	Lowestoft	Stratford-upon-Avon
Colchester Castle	Maldon Prom	Street
Coldham's Common	Markshall Estate	Swaffham
Colney Lane	Market Rasen Race.	Swansea Bay
Conwy	Malling	Thetford
Crosby	Manor Field, Whit.	The Cinder Track
Darlington South Pk.	Mersea Island	Thomas Mills
Dulwich	Mildenhall Hub	University Parks
Edinburgh	Monsal Trail	Victoria Dock
Felixstowe	Moors Valley	Wallaceneuk
Ferry Meadows	Mulbarton	Wickford Memorial
Fountains Abbey	Newark	Winchester
Fritton Lake	Northala Fields	York
Ganavan Sands	North Walsham	
Gorleston Cliffs	Norwich	Run 101: Dalby Forest

Red	Glade Runner (2020)	locations 1-50 on poetry tour
Green	Silent Running (2024)	locations 51-100 on poetry tour

APPENDIX 3. PARKRUN POET IN STATISTICS

EVENT – RUNNING	Best overall position	Best time
Norwich	178	00:25:12
Thetford	55	00:25:20
Mulbarton	30	00:25:48
Hackney Marshes	205	00:25:49
King's Lynn	129	00:25:52
Lowestoft	156	00:25:55
Rutland Water	99	00:26:05
Haverhill	13	00:26:07
Moors Valley	219	00:26:14
Lincoln	115	00:26:14
Shrewsbury	185	00:26:18
Swaffham	32	00:26:24
Felixstowe	96	00:26:26
Bushy	617	00:26:30
Chelmsford Central	290	00:26:35
York	271	00:26:38
Gorleston Cliffs	107	00:26:43
Newark	61	00:26:43
Maldon Prom	103	00:26:44
Coldham's Common	150	00:26:44
Ipswich	196	00:26:45
Littleport	70	00:26:47

Kesgrave	119	00:26:48
Great Notley	96	00:26:48
Colchester Castle	140	00:26:48
Sloughbottom	90	00:26:50
Great Dunmow	33	00:26:52
Hunstanton Promenade	30	00:26:56
Clare Castle	42	00:26:57
Brockenhurst	110	00:26:57
Severn Bridge	65	00:26:58
Catton	308	00:27:02
Blickling	113	00:27:04
Clumber Park	116	00:27:09
Billericay	126	00:27:11
Brundall	143	00:27:15
Loch Neaton, Watton	49	00:27:16
South Woodham Ferrers	44	00:27:20
Sizewell	36	00:27:23
Mersea Island	22	00:27:31
Lingwood	27	00:27:36
Clacton Seafront	38	00:27:43
Harwich	50	00:27:49
Great Cornard	61	00:27:51
Highwoods	62	00:27:53
Brandon Country Park	30	00:27:57

Colney Lane	123	00:28:12
Bury St Edmunds	119	00:28:21
Fritton Lake	35	00:28:22
Thomas Mills	51	00:28:24
Street	58	00:28:54
North Walsham	71	00:29:06
Winchester	235	00:29:13
Victoria Dock	114	00:29:14
Sheringham	77	00:29:15
The Cinder Track, Whitby	102	00:29:23
Alness	41	00:29:26
Southend	130	00:29:26
Peel	229	00:29:28
Mildenhall Hub	41	00:29:32
Manor Field, Whittlesey	44	00:29:33
Edinburgh	245	00:29:34
Wickford Memorial	84	00:29:35
Crosby	72	00:29:37
Pegwell Bay	90	00:29:38
Conwy	131	00:29:40
Cassiobury	245	00:29:42
Darlington South Park	179	00:29:43
Market Rasen Racecourse	46	00:29:49
University Parks	248	00:29:50

Roding Valley	80	00:29:52
Malling	92	00:29:52
Southwark	281	00:29:53
Swansea Bay	257	00:29:56
Monsal Trail	129	00:29:57
Northala Fields	171	00:30:04
Ferry Meadows	252	00:30:08
Belton House	171	00:30:13
Dulwich	419	00:30:15
Wallaceneuk	30	00:30:20
Dalby Forest	100	00:30:22
Harleston Magpies	41	00:30:24
Burgess	344	00:30:25
Humber Bridge	64	00:30:28
Harrogate	173	00:30:30
Storeys Field	280	00:30:33
Soham Village College	32	00:30:42
Stratford-upon-Avon	218	00:30:48
Rendlesham Forest	70	00:31:01
Chalkwell Beach	239	00:31:03
Sewerby	137	00:31:11
Chilton Fields	77	00:31:28
Alton Water	30	00:31:38
Shorne Woods	141	00:31:44

Markshall Estate	128	00:31:51
Fountains Abbey	361	00:32:16
Castle Park	169	00:32:44
Sandringham	109	00:32:46
Great Yarmouth North Beach	84	00:33:41
Ganavan Sands	67	00:33:47
Royal Tunbridge Wells	137	00:34:12
BEST	13	00:25:12

SPEED WALKING

Harwich	108	00:39:12
King's Lynn	269	00:40:28
Gorleston Cliffs	293	00:41:45
Bury St. Edmunds	233	00:44:48
Maldon Prom	207	00:44:51
Town Moor	502	00:45:46
Aviemore	110	00:46:21
Monsal Trail	273	00:47:20
BEST	108	00:39:12

Banksy artwork at Gorleston Cliffs parkrun intrigues my son

The parkrun poet with Paralympian Noel Thatcher, Castle Park

Manufactured by Amazon.ca
Bolton, ON